A WHO HQ GRAPHIC NOVEL

# Who Sparked the Montgomery Bus Boycott?

## ROSA PARKS

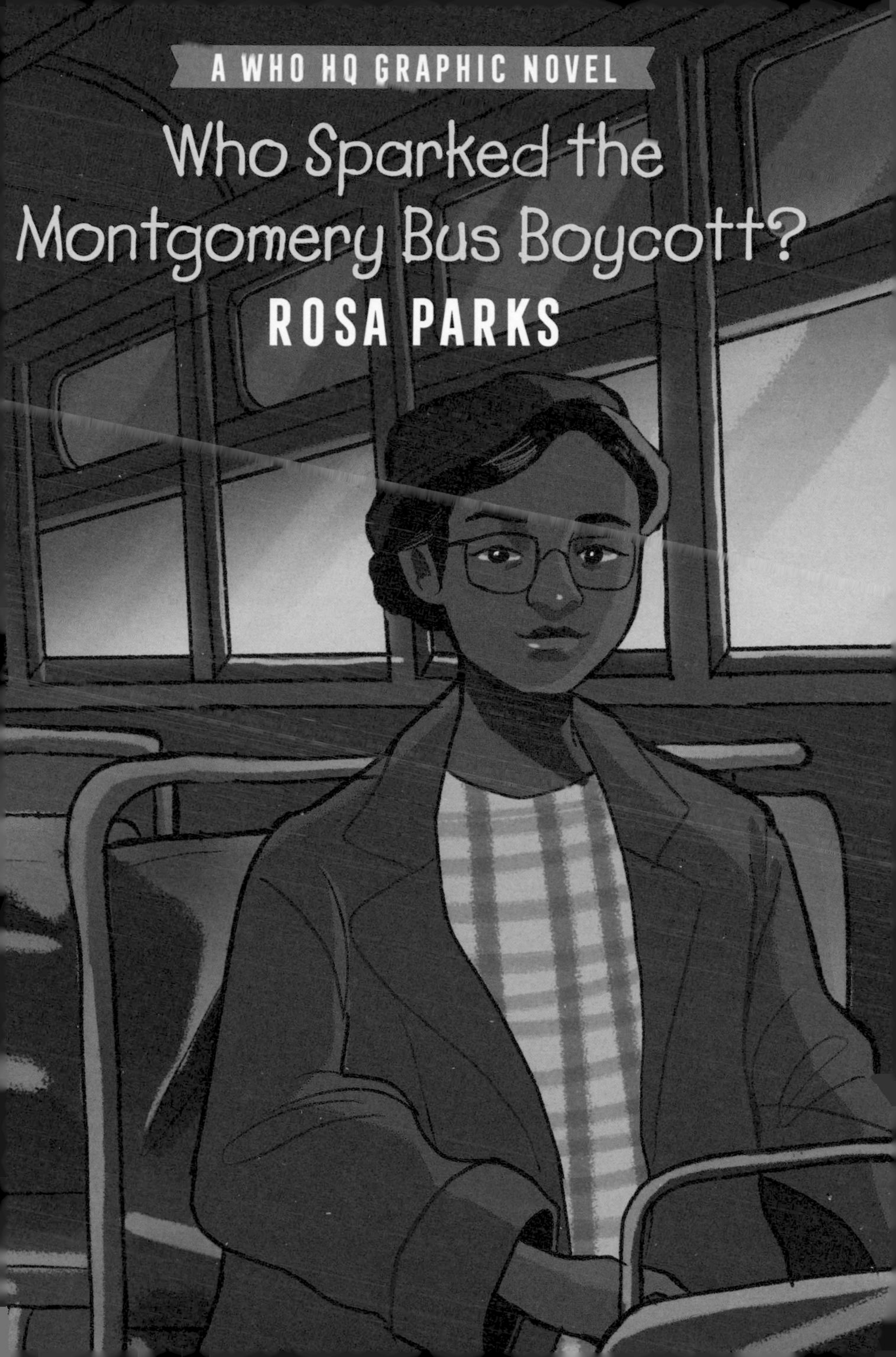

To my parents. To Rosa. Be humble. Be kind—IF

To my family, friends, and community—AH

PENGUIN WORKSHOP
An Imprint of Penguin Random House LLC, New York

Penguin supports copyright. Copyright fuels creativity, encourages diverse voices, promotes free speech, and creates a vibrant culture. Thank you for buying an authorized edition of this book and for complying with copyright laws by not reproducing, scanning, or distributing any part of it in any form without permission. You are supporting writers and allowing Penguin to continue to publish books for every reader.

The publisher does not have any control over and does not assume any responsibility for author or third-party websites or their content.

Copyright © 2021 by Penguin Random House LLC. All rights reserved.
Published by Penguin Workshop, an imprint of Penguin Random House LLC, New York.
PENGUIN and PENGUIN WORKSHOP are trademarks of Penguin Books Ltd.
WHO HQ & Design is a registered trademark of Penguin Random House LLC.
Manufactured in China.

Visit us online at www.penguinrandomhouse.com.

Library of Congress Cataloging-in-Publication Data is available upon request.

ISBN 9780593224465 (pbk)                    10 9 8 7 6 5 4 3 2 1 HH
ISBN 9780593224472 (hc)                     10 9 8 7 6 5 4 3 2 1 HH

Lettering by Comicraft
Book design by Jay Emmanuel

This is a work of nonfiction. All of the events that unfold in the narrative are rooted in historical fact. Some dialogue and characters have been fictionalized in order to illustrate or teach a historical point.

For more information about your favorite historical figures, places, and events, please visit www.whohq.com

A WHO HQ GRAPHIC NOVEL

# Who Sparked the Montgomery Bus Boycott?

## ROSA PARKS

by Insha Fitzpatrick
illustrated by Abelle Hayford
colors by Hanna Schroy

Penguin Workshop

# Introduction

Rosa Parks looked at her watch as she waited for the Cleveland Avenue bus at the corner of Montgomery and Moulton Streets in Montgomery, Alabama. It was Thursday, December 1, 1955, and forty-two-year-old Rosa wanted to go home after a long day of working as a seamstress. She'd been in Montgomery for twenty years, after spending her childhood on her grandparents' farm in Pine Level, Alabama, with her mother, Leona, and brother, Sylvester. But even though Montgomery was her home, she still didn't feel welcome there.

In the 1950s, Montgomery (and much of the American South) had unfair laws, known as Jim Crow laws. These laws made it so Black people were "separate but equal" from white people. There were a large number of places—including movie theaters, restaurants, churches, and even schools—where Black people could not go, or places they were separated from because of the color of their skin. Montgomery's bus system operated under these rules, and buses were divided into sections: a white section, a Black and white section, and a Black section. If a white passenger got on the bus and the bus was full, a Black passenger had to give up their seat for them.

As the Cleveland Avenue bus came to a halt, Rosa and the other passengers lined up to pay their fare. Rosa quickly boarded the bus and found a seat in the section meant for Black and white passengers. With every stop, the bus began to fill up. A few stops later, a white man stepped onto the bus, and the bus driver, James Blake, noticing there were no available seats, demanded that Rosa and three other Black passengers give up their seats and move to the back. As the three passengers began to move to the back, Rosa stayed seated.

Blake grew angrier by the second, his voice booming louder and louder. "Are you going to stand up?" Blake asked. Not moving an inch, Rosa looked straight at him and simply said, "No." "Well, I'm going to have you arrested," Blake barked. And Rosa, still sitting in her seat, calmly replied, "You may do that."

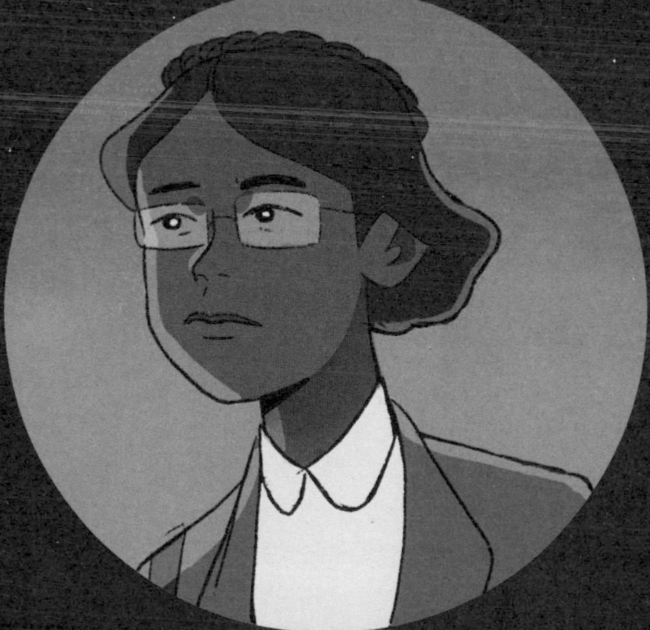

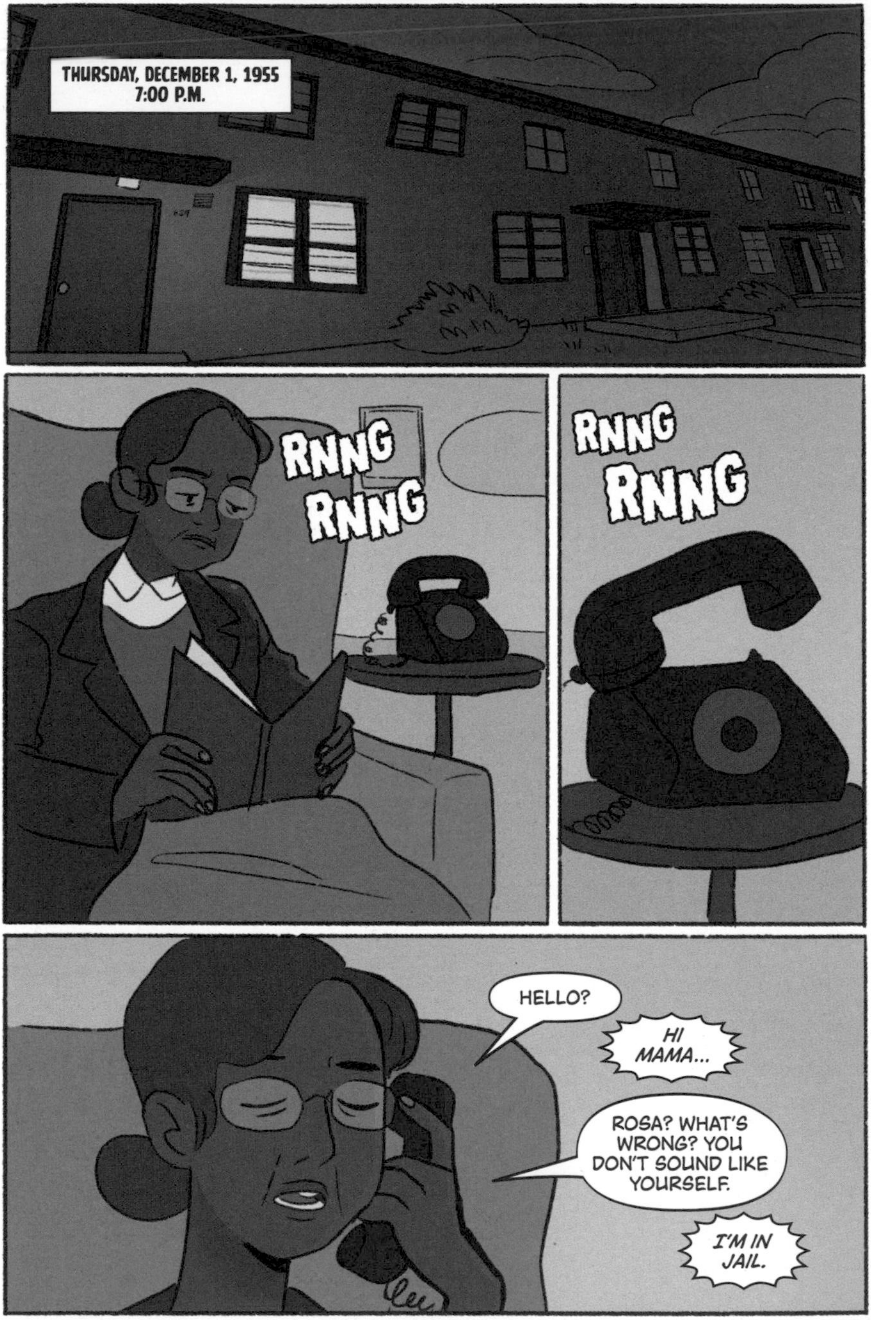
THURSDAY, DECEMBER 1, 1955
7:00 P.M.
RNNG RNNG
RNNG RNNG
HELLO?
HI MAMA...
ROSA? WHAT'S WRONG? YOU DON'T SOUND LIKE YOURSELF.
I'M IN JAIL.

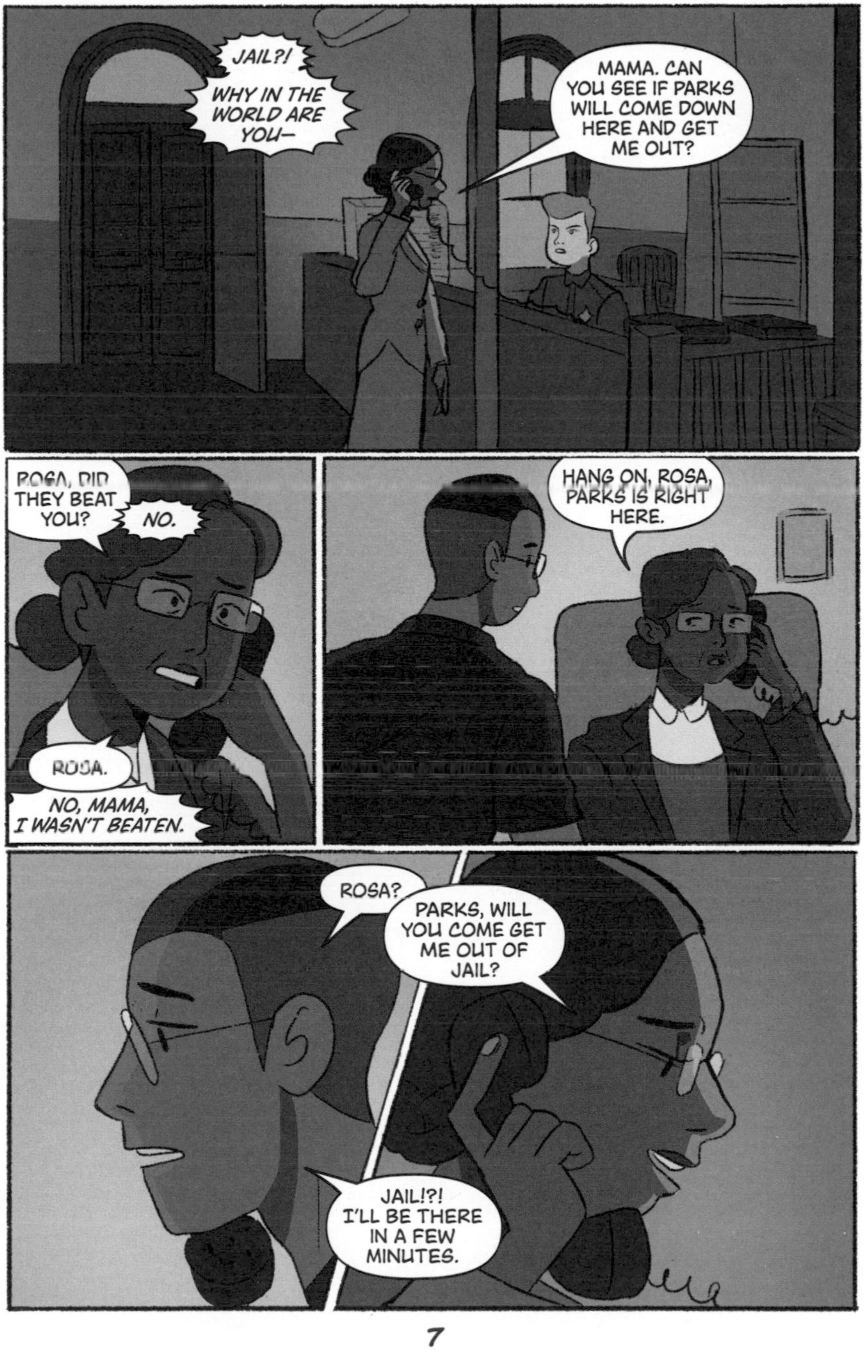
JAIL?!
WHY IN THE WORLD ARE YOU—
MAMA. CAN YOU SEE IF PARKS WILL COME DOWN HERE AND GET ME OUT?
ROSA, DID THEY BEAT YOU?
NO.
ROSA.
NO, MAMA, I WASN'T BEATEN.
HANG ON, ROSA, PARKS IS RIGHT HERE.
ROSA?
PARKS, WILL YOU COME GET ME OUT OF JAIL?
JAIL!?!
I'LL BE THERE IN A FEW MINUTES.

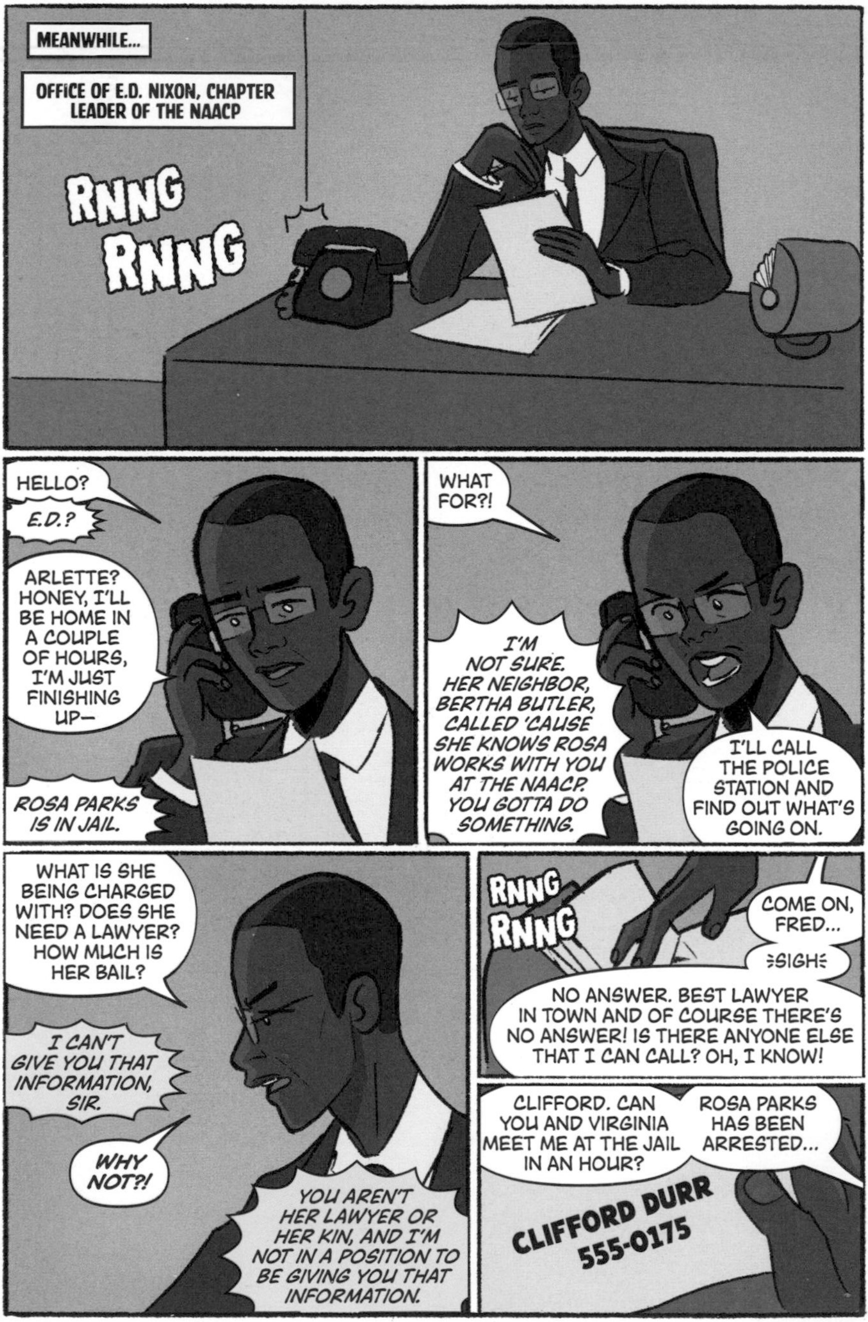
MEANWHILE...
OFFICE OF E.D. NIXON, CHAPTER LEADER OF THE NAACP
RNNG RNNG
HELLO?
E.D.?
ARLETTE? HONEY, I'LL BE HOME IN A COUPLE OF HOURS, I'M JUST FINISHING UP—
ROSA PARKS IS IN JAIL.
WHAT FOR?!
I'M NOT SURE. HER NEIGHBOR, BERTHA BUTLER, CALLED 'CAUSE SHE KNOWS ROSA WORKS WITH YOU AT THE NAACP. YOU GOTTA DO SOMETHING.
I'LL CALL THE POLICE STATION AND FIND OUT WHAT'S GOING ON.
WHAT IS SHE BEING CHARGED WITH? DOES SHE NEED A LAWYER? HOW MUCH IS HER BAIL?
I CAN'T GIVE YOU THAT INFORMATION, SIR.
WHY NOT?!
YOU AREN'T HER LAWYER OR HER KIN, AND I'M NOT IN A POSITION TO BE GIVING YOU THAT INFORMATION.
RNNG RNNG
COME ON, FRED...
SIGH
NO ANSWER. BEST LAWYER IN TOWN AND OF COURSE THERE'S NO ANSWER! IS THERE ANYONE ELSE THAT I CAN CALL? OH, I KNOW!
CLIFFORD. CAN YOU AND VIRGINIA MEET ME AT THE JAIL IN AN HOUR?
ROSA PARKS HAS BEEN ARRESTED...
CLIFFORD DURR 555-0175

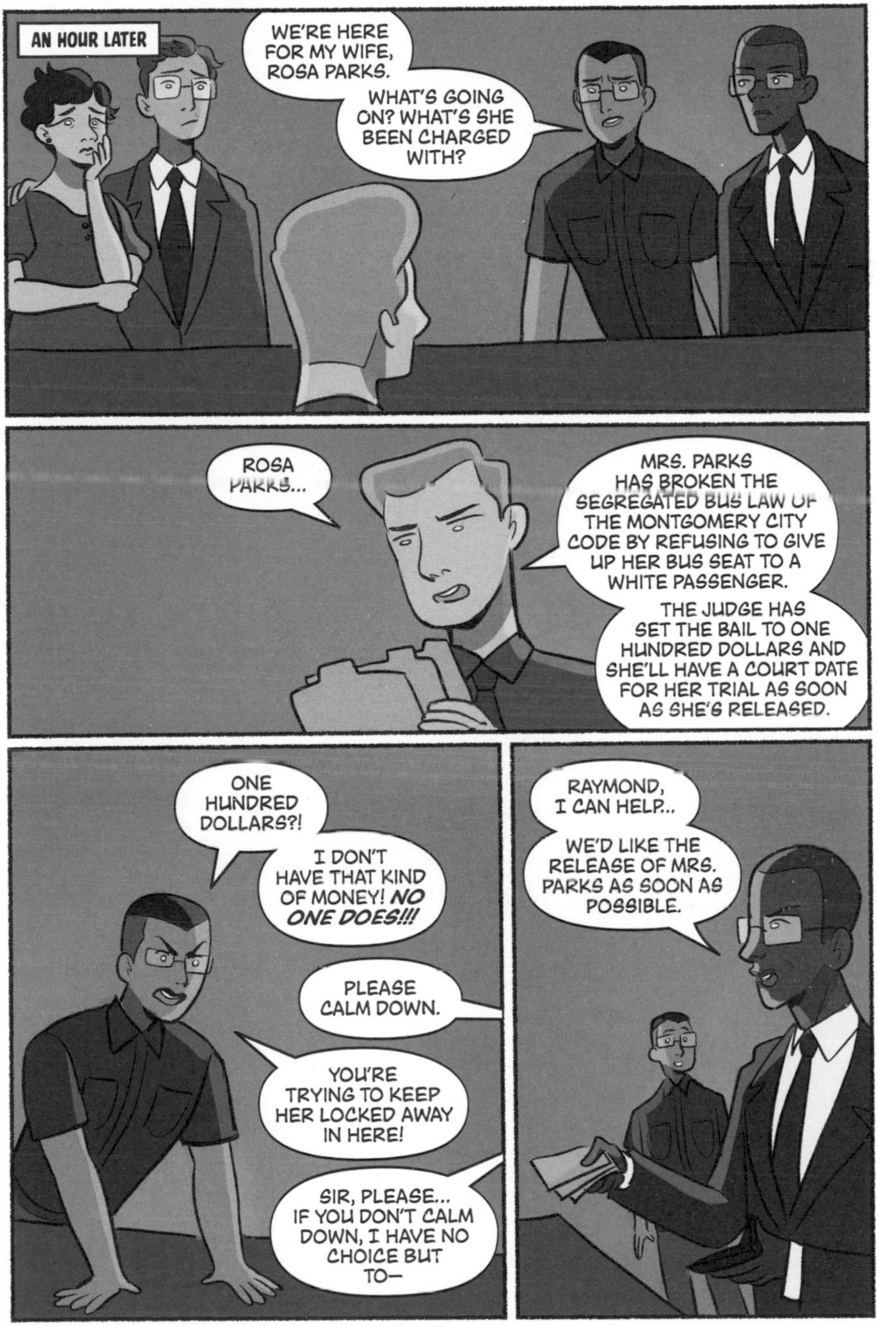
AN HOUR LATER
WE'RE HERE FOR MY WIFE, ROSA PARKS.
WHAT'S GOING ON? WHAT'S SHE BEEN CHARGED WITH?
ROSA PARKS...
MRS. PARKS HAS BROKEN THE SEGREGATED BUS LAW OF THE MONTGOMERY CITY CODE BY REFUSING TO GIVE UP HER BUS SEAT TO A WHITE PASSENGER.
THE JUDGE HAS SET THE BAIL TO ONE HUNDRED DOLLARS AND SHE'LL HAVE A COURT DATE FOR HER TRIAL AS SOON AS SHE'S RELEASED.
ONE HUNDRED DOLLARS?!
I DON'T HAVE THAT KIND OF MONEY! *NO ONE DOES!!!*
PLEASE CALM DOWN.
YOU'RE TRYING TO KEEP HER LOCKED AWAY IN HERE!
SIR, PLEASE... IF YOU DON'T CALM DOWN, I HAVE NO CHOICE BUT TO—
RAYMOND, I CAN HELP...
WE'D LIKE THE RELEASE OF MRS. PARKS AS SOON AS POSSIBLE.

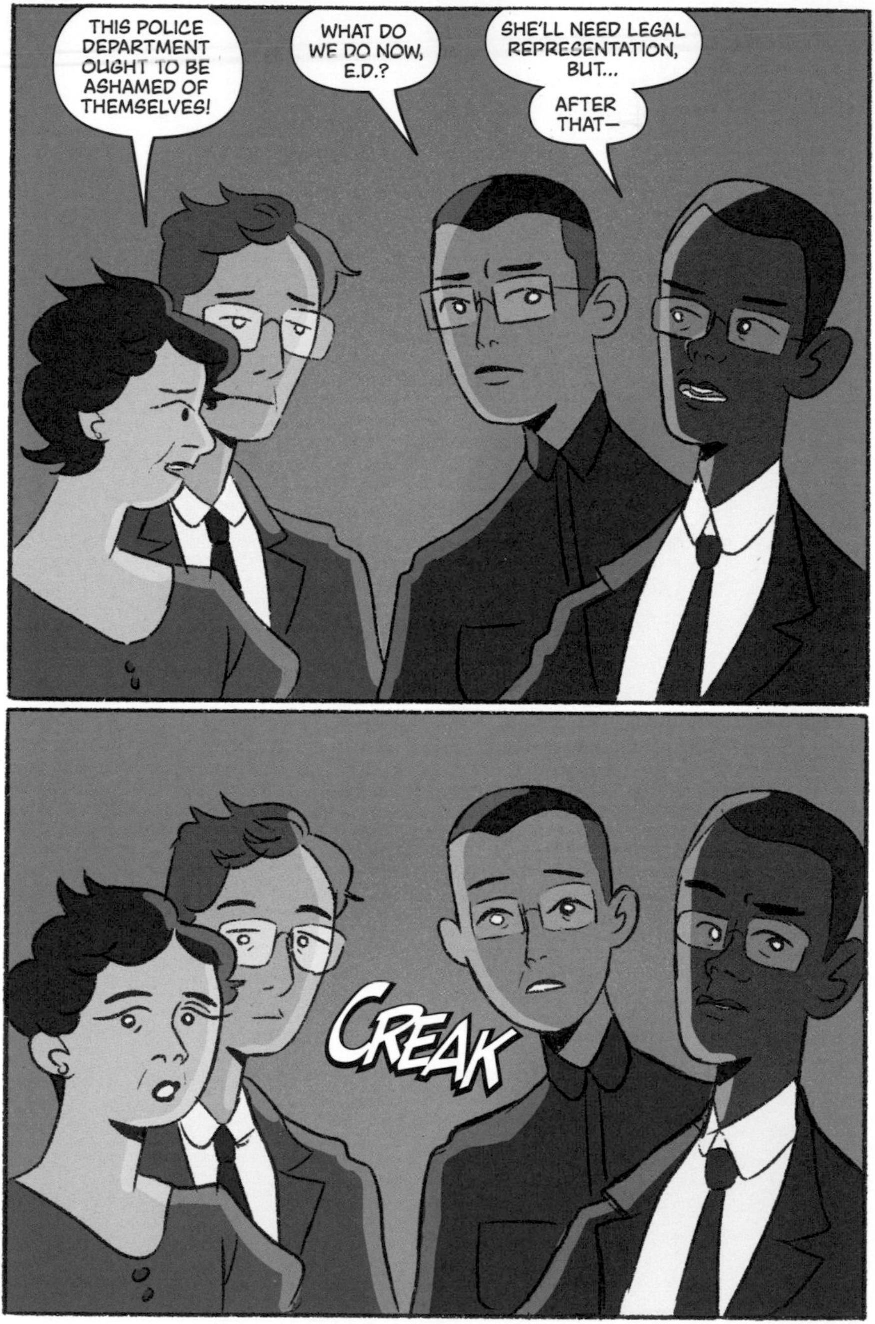
THIS POLICE DEPARTMENT OUGHT TO BE ASHAMED OF THEMSELVES!
WHAT DO WE DO NOW, E.D.?
SHE'LL NEED LEGAL REPRESENTATION, BUT...
AFTER THAT—
CREAK

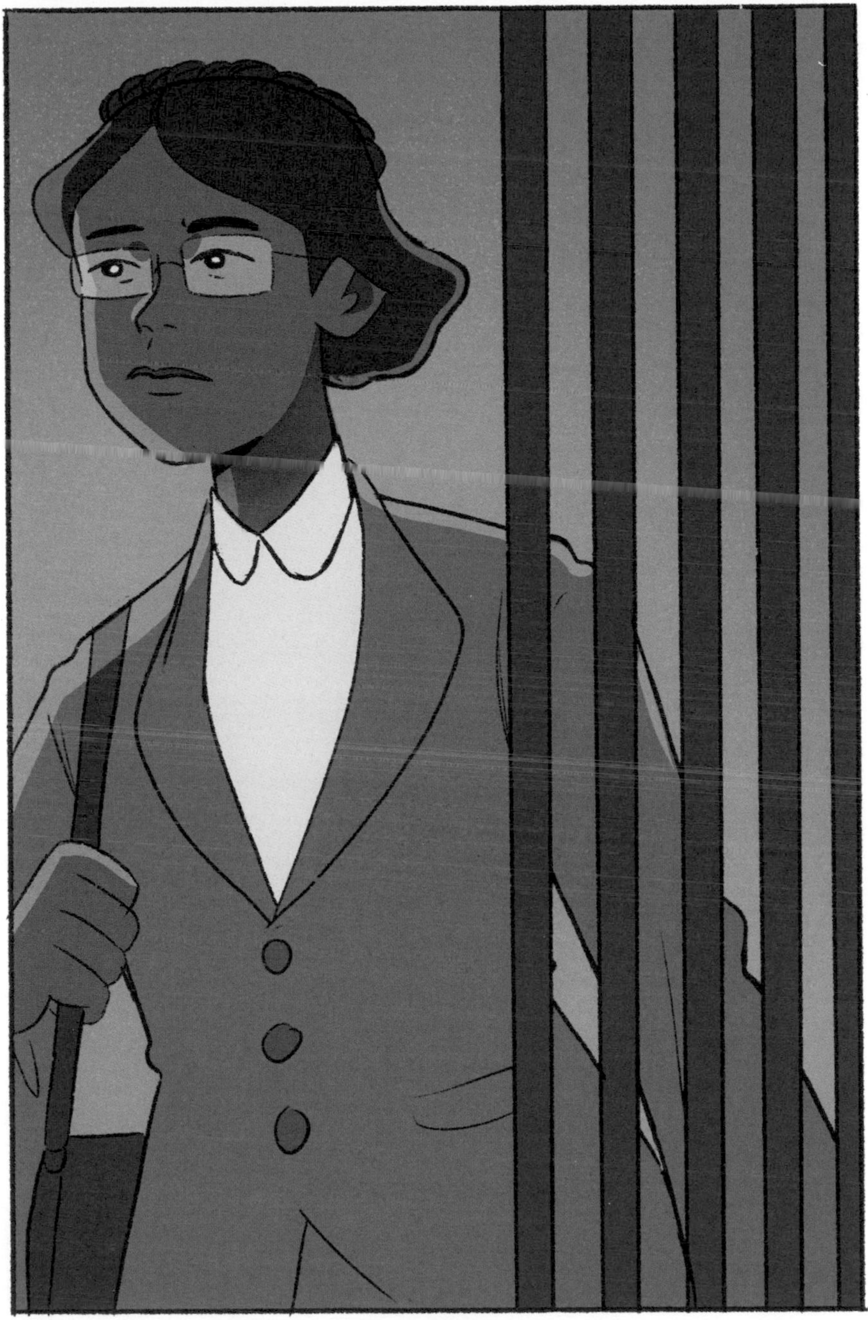

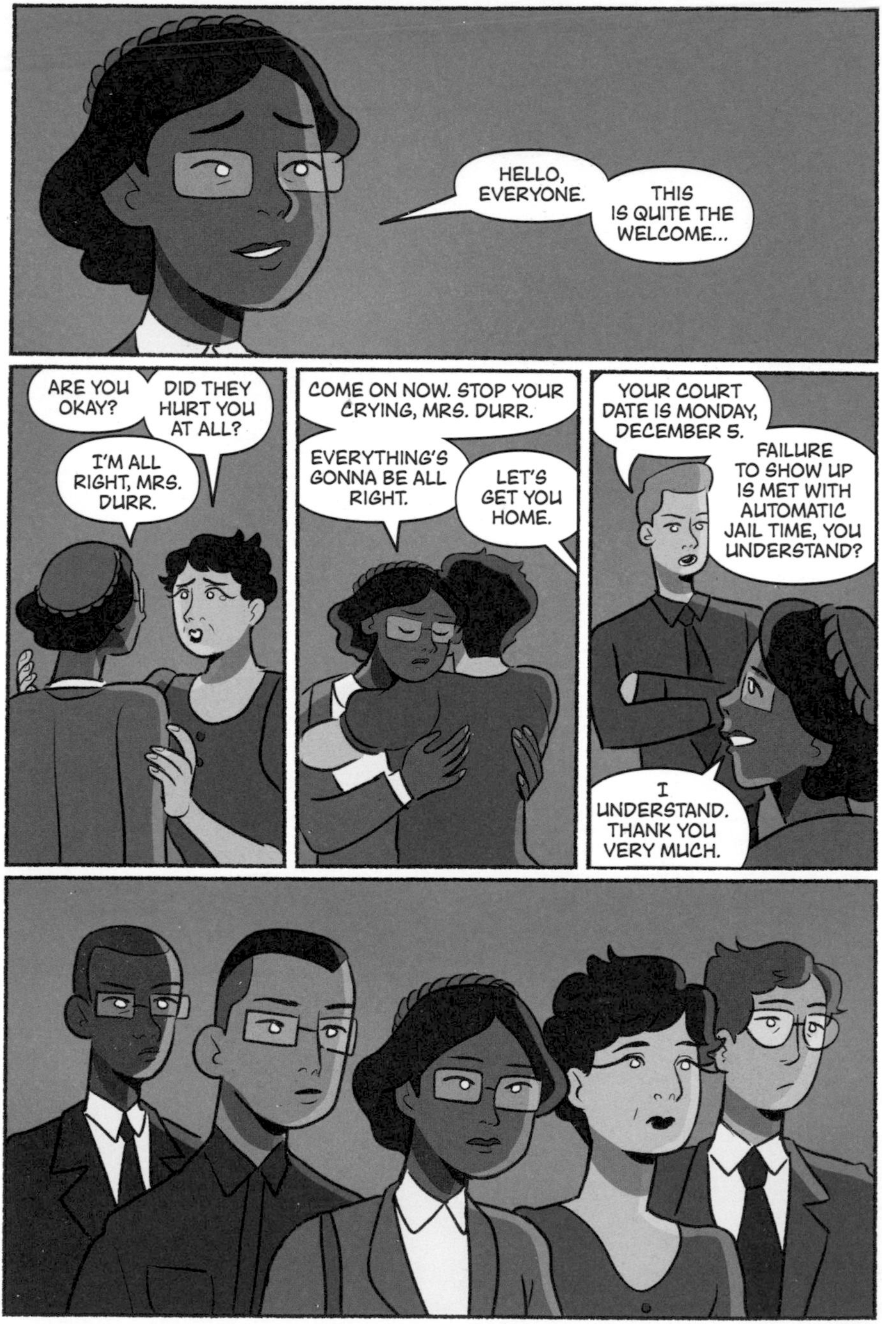
HELLO, EVERYONE.
THIS IS QUITE THE WELCOME...
ARE YOU OKAY?
DID THEY HURT YOU AT ALL?
I'M ALL RIGHT, MRS. DURR.
COME ON NOW. STOP YOUR CRYING, MRS. DURR.
EVERYTHING'S GONNA BE ALL RIGHT.
LET'S GET YOU HOME.
YOUR COURT DATE IS MONDAY, DECEMBER 5.
FAILURE TO SHOW UP IS MET WITH AUTOMATIC JAIL TIME, YOU UNDERSTAND?
I UNDERSTAND. THANK YOU VERY MUCH.

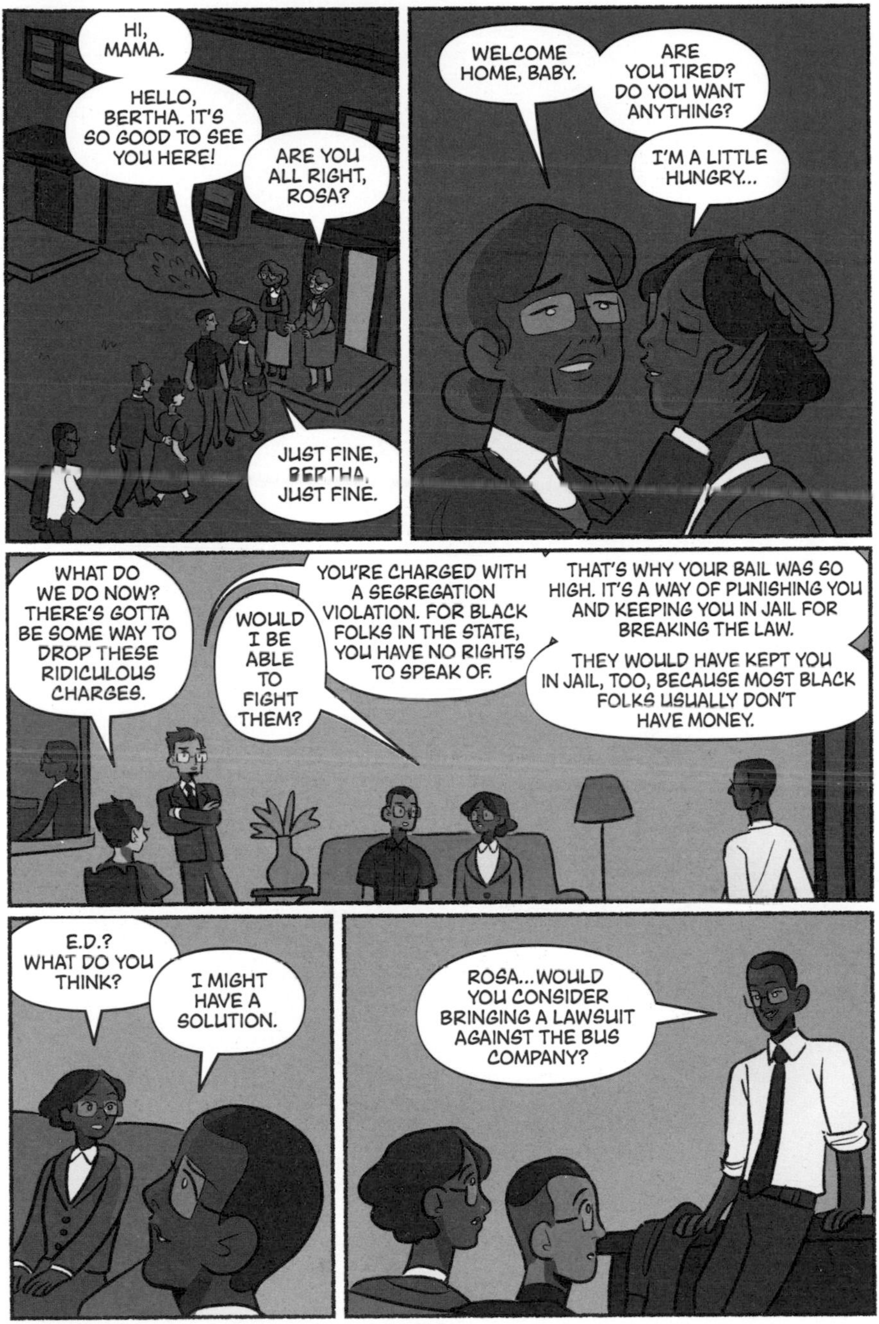
HI, MAMA.
HELLO, BERTHA. IT'S SO GOOD TO SEE YOU HERE!
ARE YOU ALL RIGHT, ROSA?
JUST FINE, BERTHA, JUST FINE.
WELCOME HOME, BABY.
ARE YOU TIRED? DO YOU WANT ANYTHING?
I'M A LITTLE HUNGRY...
WHAT DO WE DO NOW? THERE'S GOTTA BE SOME WAY TO DROP THESE RIDICULOUS CHARGES.
WOULD I BE ABLE TO FIGHT THEM?
YOU'RE CHARGED WITH A SEGREGATION VIOLATION. FOR BLACK FOLKS IN THE STATE, YOU HAVE NO RIGHTS TO SPEAK OF.
THAT'S WHY YOUR BAIL WAS SO HIGH. IT'S A WAY OF PUNISHING YOU AND KEEPING YOU IN JAIL FOR BREAKING THE LAW.
THEY WOULD HAVE KEPT YOU IN JAIL, TOO, BECAUSE MOST BLACK FOLKS USUALLY DON'T HAVE MONEY.
E.D.? WHAT DO YOU THINK?
I MIGHT HAVE A SOLUTION.
ROSA...WOULD YOU CONSIDER BRINGING A LAWSUIT AGAINST THE BUS COMPANY?

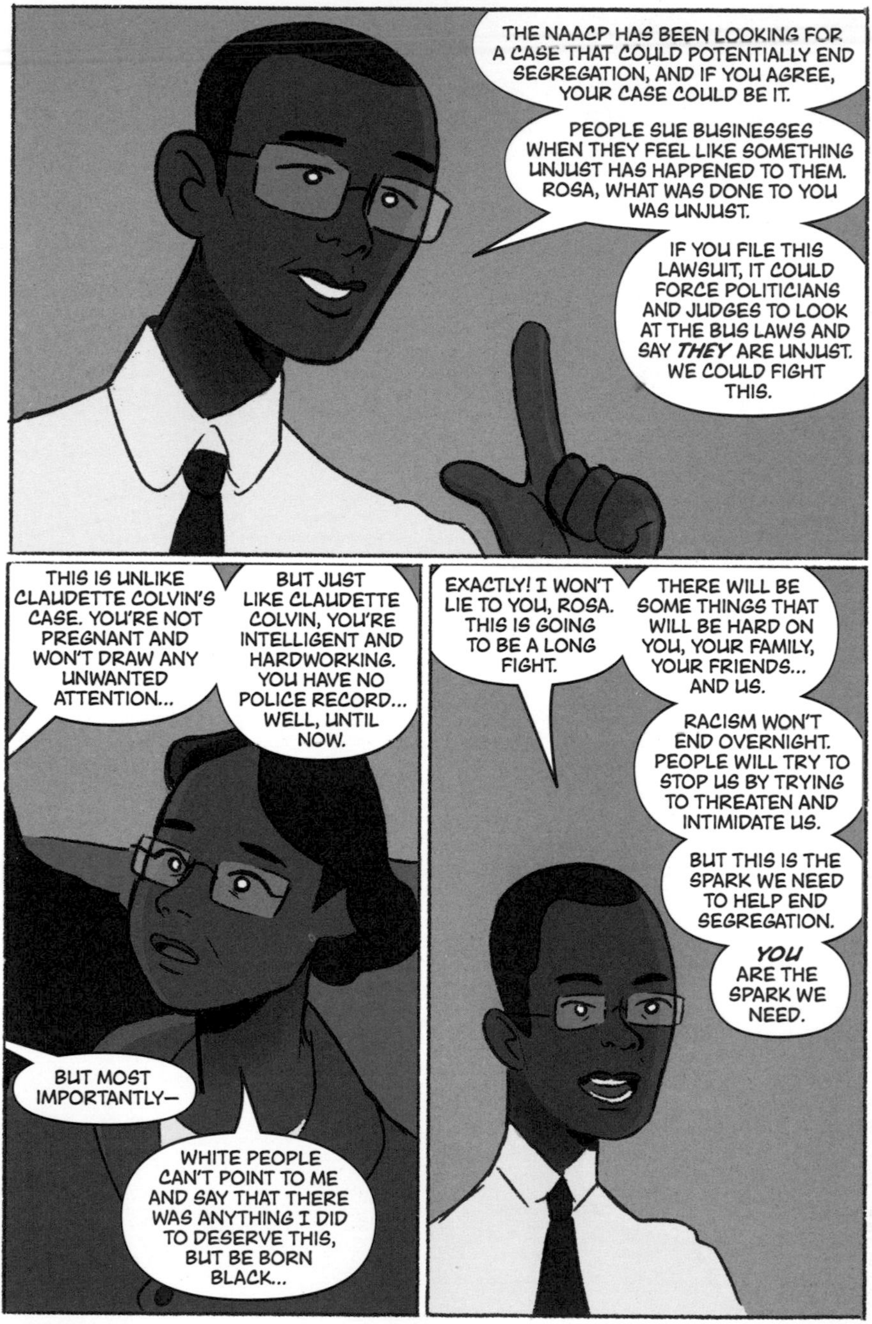
THE NAACP HAS BEEN LOOKING FOR A CASE THAT COULD POTENTIALLY END SEGREGATION, AND IF YOU AGREE, YOUR CASE COULD BE IT.
PEOPLE SUE BUSINESSES WHEN THEY FEEL LIKE SOMETHING UNJUST HAS HAPPENED TO THEM. ROSA, WHAT WAS DONE TO YOU WAS UNJUST.
IF YOU FILE THIS LAWSUIT, IT COULD FORCE POLITICIANS AND JUDGES TO LOOK AT THE BUS LAWS AND SAY *THEY* ARE UNJUST. WE COULD FIGHT THIS.
THIS IS UNLIKE CLAUDETTE COLVIN'S CASE. YOU'RE NOT PREGNANT AND WON'T DRAW ANY UNWANTED ATTENTION...
BUT JUST LIKE CLAUDETTE COLVIN, YOU'RE INTELLIGENT AND HARDWORKING. YOU HAVE NO POLICE RECORD... WELL, UNTIL NOW.
BUT MOST IMPORTANTLY—
WHITE PEOPLE CAN'T POINT TO ME AND SAY THAT THERE WAS ANYTHING I DID TO DESERVE THIS, BUT BE BORN BLACK...
EXACTLY! I WON'T LIE TO YOU, ROSA. THIS IS GOING TO BE A LONG FIGHT.
THERE WILL BE SOME THINGS THAT WILL BE HARD ON YOU, YOUR FAMILY, YOUR FRIENDS... AND US.
RACISM WON'T END OVERNIGHT. PEOPLE WILL TRY TO STOP US BY TRYING TO THREATEN AND INTIMIDATE US.
BUT THIS IS THE SPARK WE NEED TO HELP END SEGREGATION.
*YOU* ARE THE SPARK WE NEED.

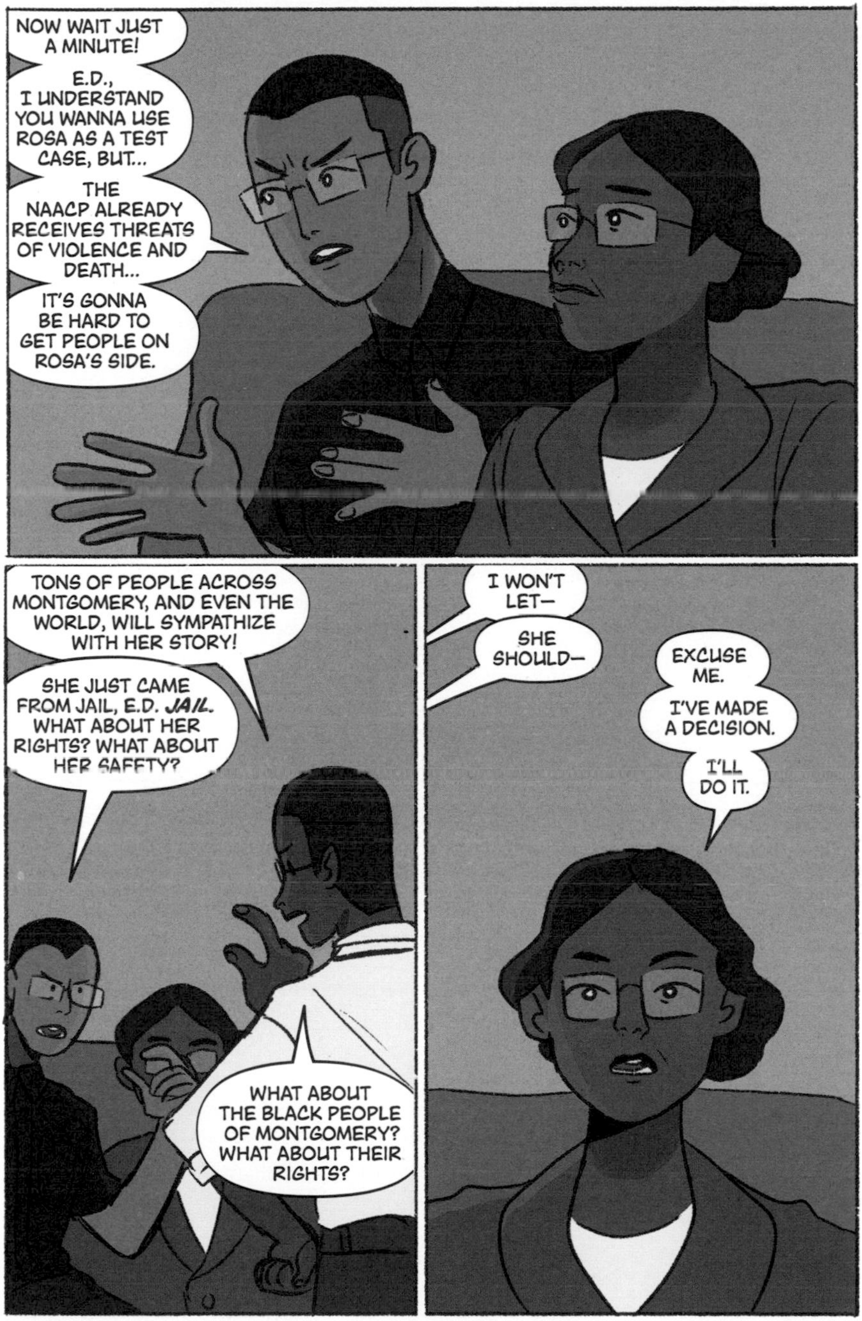
NOW WAIT JUST A MINUTE!
E.D., I UNDERSTAND YOU WANNA USE ROSA AS A TEST CASE, BUT...
THE NAACP ALREADY RECEIVES THREATS OF VIOLENCE AND DEATH...
IT'S GONNA BE HARD TO GET PEOPLE ON ROSA'S SIDE.
TONS OF PEOPLE ACROSS MONTGOMERY, AND EVEN THE WORLD, WILL SYMPATHIZE WITH HER STORY!
SHE JUST CAME FROM JAIL, E.D. *JAIL.* WHAT ABOUT HER RIGHTS? WHAT ABOUT HER SAFETY?
WHAT ABOUT THE BLACK PEOPLE OF MONTGOMERY? WHAT ABOUT THEIR RIGHTS?
I WON'T LET—
SHE SHOULD—
EXCUSE ME.
I'VE MADE A DECISION.
I'LL DO IT.

16

## Jim Crow Laws

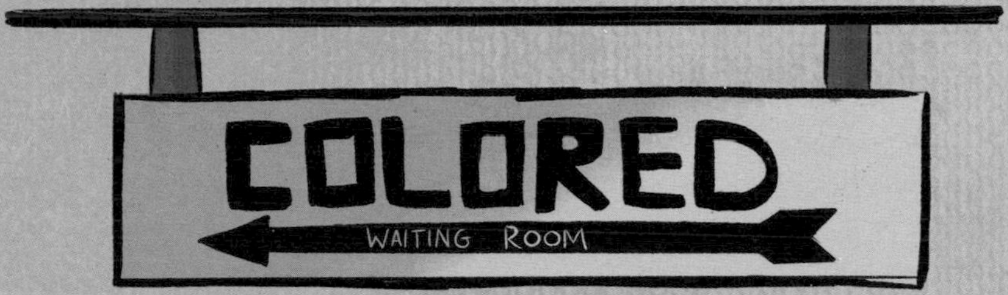
COLORED
WAITING ROOM

After the Thirteenth Amendment to the US Constitution was signed into law in December of 1865, states in the American South quickly created laws that made it legal to separate people by race. They were known as Jim Crow laws. These laws prohibited Black people from going to the same restaurants, attending the same schools, or even sitting in the same sections of the bus. Jim Crow laws also made voting harder for Black people by enforcing hard literacy tests and an expensive voting tax (called a poll tax), which most people couldn't afford.

In 1954, the Supreme Court case of *Brown v. Board of Education* declared Jim Crow laws unconstitutional. Ten years later, Jim Crow laws were made illegal by the Civil Rights Act of 1964 and the Voting Rights Act of 1965.

18

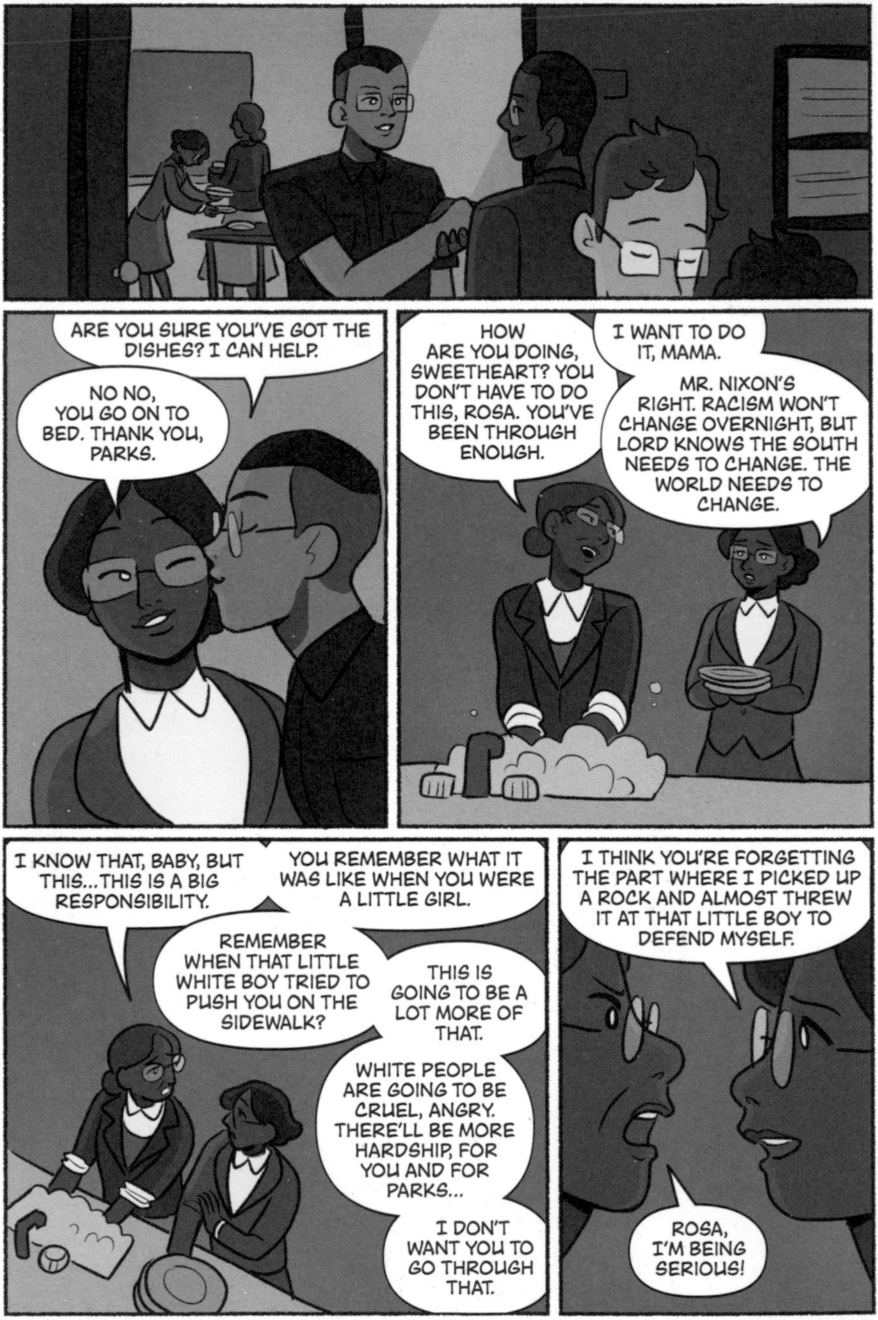

ARE YOU SURE YOU'VE GOT THE DISHES? I CAN HELP.
NO NO, YOU GO ON TO BED. THANK YOU, PARKS.
HOW ARE YOU DOING, SWEETHEART? YOU DON'T HAVE TO DO THIS, ROSA. YOU'VE BEEN THROUGH ENOUGH.
I WANT TO DO IT, MAMA.
MR. NIXON'S RIGHT. RACISM WON'T CHANGE OVERNIGHT, BUT LORD KNOWS THE SOUTH NEEDS TO CHANGE. THE WORLD NEEDS TO CHANGE.
I KNOW THAT, BABY, BUT THIS...THIS IS A BIG RESPONSIBILITY.
YOU REMEMBER WHAT IT WAS LIKE WHEN YOU WERE A LITTLE GIRL.
REMEMBER WHEN THAT LITTLE WHITE BOY TRIED TO PUSH YOU ON THE SIDEWALK?
THIS IS GOING TO BE A LOT MORE OF THAT.
WHITE PEOPLE ARE GOING TO BE CRUEL, ANGRY. THERE'LL BE MORE HARDSHIP, FOR YOU AND FOR PARKS...
I DON'T WANT YOU TO GO THROUGH THAT.
I THINK YOU'RE FORGETTING THE PART WHERE I PICKED UP A ROCK AND ALMOST THREW IT AT THAT LITTLE BOY TO DEFEND MYSELF.
ROSA, I'M BEING SERIOUS!

21

23

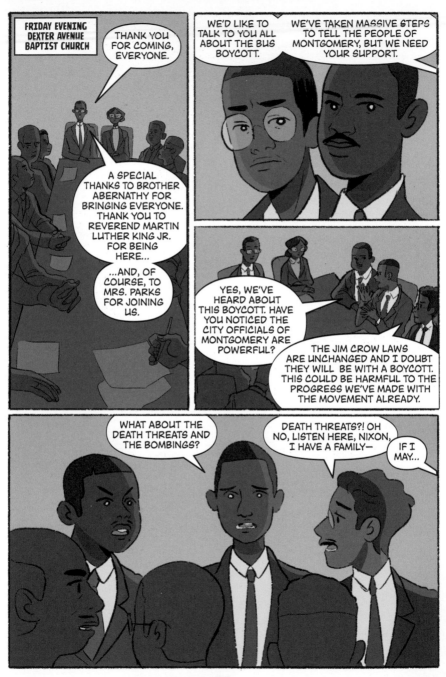

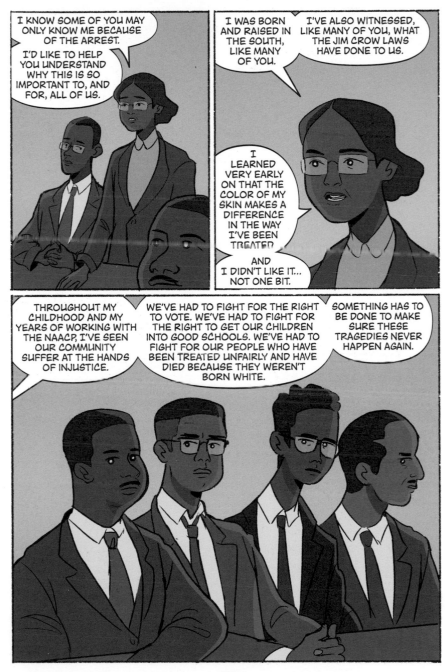

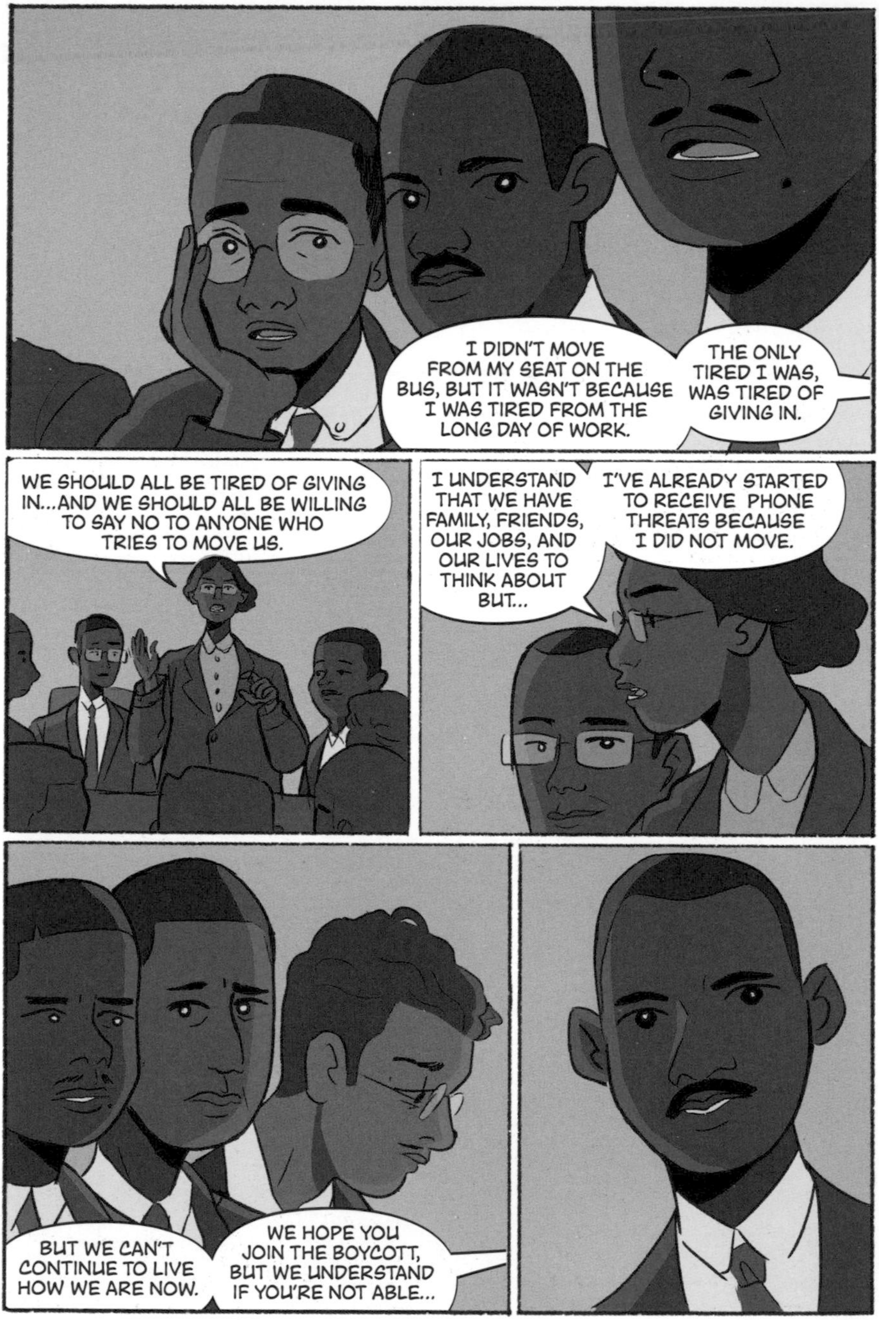
I DIDN'T MOVE FROM MY SEAT ON THE BUS, BUT IT WASN'T BECAUSE I WAS TIRED FROM THE LONG DAY OF WORK.
THE ONLY TIRED I WAS, WAS TIRED OF GIVING IN.
WE SHOULD ALL BE TIRED OF GIVING IN...AND WE SHOULD ALL BE WILLING TO SAY NO TO ANYONE WHO TRIES TO MOVE US.
I UNDERSTAND THAT WE HAVE FAMILY, FRIENDS, OUR JOBS, AND OUR LIVES TO THINK ABOUT BUT...
I'VE ALREADY STARTED TO RECEIVE PHONE THREATS BECAUSE I DID NOT MOVE.
BUT WE CAN'T CONTINUE TO LIVE HOW WE ARE NOW.
WE HOPE YOU JOIN THE BOYCOTT, BUT WE UNDERSTAND IF YOU'RE NOT ABLE...

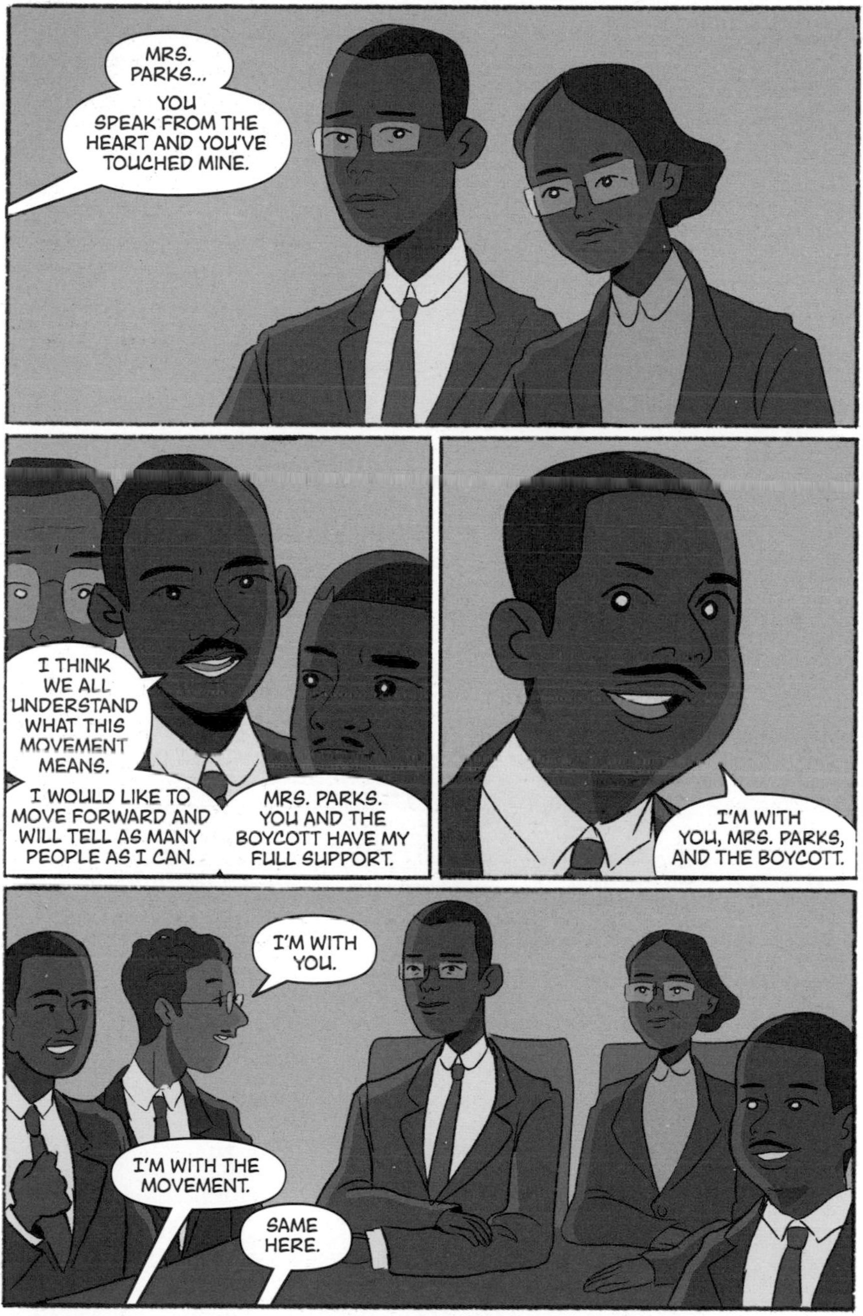
MRS. PARKS...
YOU SPEAK FROM THE HEART AND YOU'VE TOUCHED MINE.
I THINK WE ALL UNDERSTAND WHAT THIS MOVEMENT MEANS.
I WOULD LIKE TO MOVE FORWARD AND WILL TELL AS MANY PEOPLE AS I CAN.
MRS. PARKS. YOU AND THE BOYCOTT HAVE MY FULL SUPPORT.
I'M WITH YOU, MRS. PARKS, AND THE BOYCOTT.
I'M WITH YOU.
I'M WITH THE MOVEMENT.
SAME HERE.

# Martin Luther King Jr.

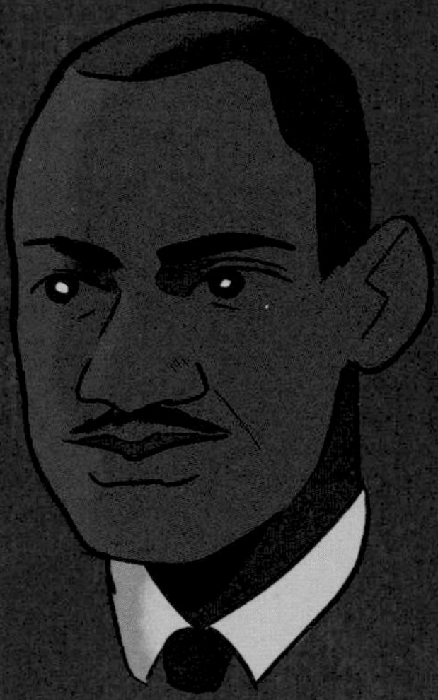

Born in Atlanta, Georgia, on January 15, 1929, Martin Luther King Jr. was a minister and civil rights activist. Martin was born into a religious family who gave him the Christian values he would come to display when it came to his activism. He encouraged his fellow activists to practice nonviolent protests.

Martin Luther King Jr. became a force for African American rights in the South, starting with the Montgomery Bus Boycott. From there, he was the president of the Southern Christian Leadership Conference, which allowed him to participate actively in planning many nonviolent protests. The largest and most famous was the March on Washington (1963) to achieve both civil and economic rights for African Americans. There, King would deliver his most famous speech, "I Have a Dream," to over 200,000 people.

Martin Luther King Jr. was a pivotal person in the civil rights movement. His words and actions helped inspire many people to fight for civil liberties. Tragically, Martin Luther King Jr. was shot to death in Memphis, Tennessee, on April 4, 1968.

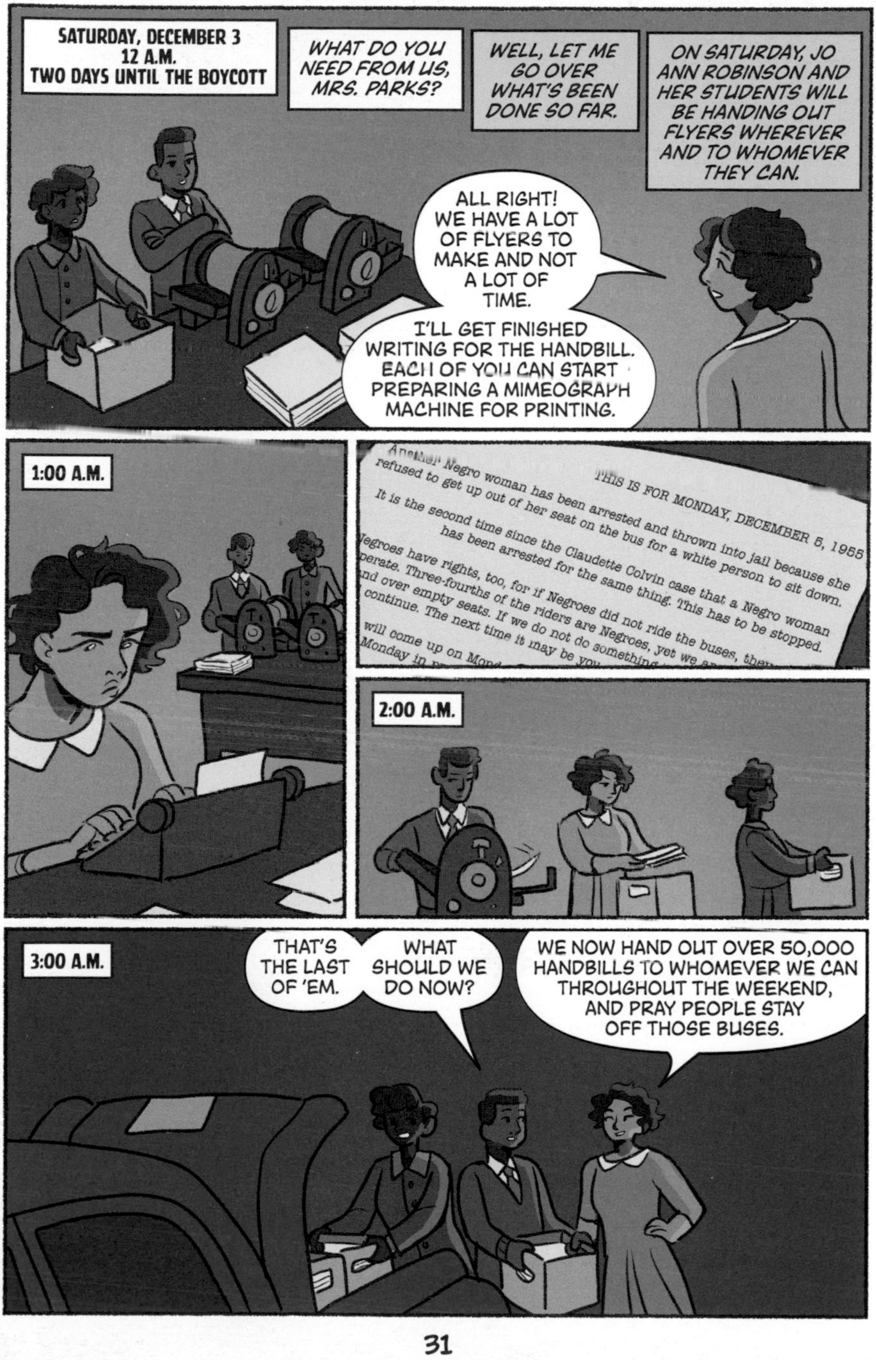
SATURDAY, DECEMBER 3
12 A.M.
TWO DAYS UNTIL THE BOYCOTT
WHAT DO YOU NEED FROM US, MRS. PARKS?
WELL, LET ME GO OVER WHAT'S BEEN DONE SO FAR.
ON SATURDAY, JO ANN ROBINSON AND HER STUDENTS WILL BE HANDING OUT FLYERS WHEREVER AND TO WHOMEVER THEY CAN.
ALL RIGHT! WE HAVE A LOT OF FLYERS TO MAKE AND NOT A LOT OF TIME.
I'LL GET FINISHED WRITING FOR THE HANDBILL. EACH OF YOU CAN START PREPARING A MIMEOGRAPH MACHINE FOR PRINTING.
1:00 A.M.
THIS IS FOR MONDAY, DECEMBER 5, 1955
Negro woman has been arrested and thrown into jail because she
refused to get up out of her seat on the bus for a white person to sit down.
It is the second time since the Claudette Colvin case that a Negro woman
has been arrested for the same thing. This has to be stopped.
egroes have rights, too, for if Negroes did not ride the buses, the
perate. Three-fourths of the riders are Negroes, yet we a
nd over empty seats. If we do not do something
continue. The next time it may be you
will come up on Mon
Monday in
2:00 A.M.
3:00 A.M.
THAT'S THE LAST OF 'EM.
WHAT SHOULD WE DO NOW?
WE NOW HAND OUT OVER 50,000 HANDBILLS TO WHOMEVER WE CAN THROUGHOUT THE WEEKEND, AND PRAY PEOPLE STAY OFF THOSE BUSES.

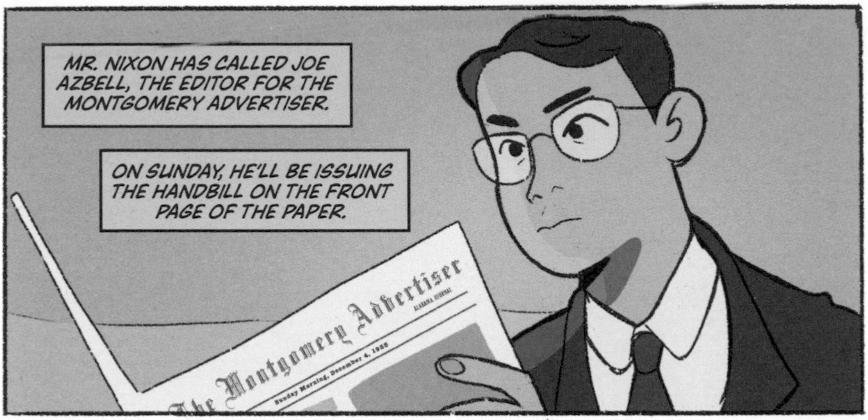

MR. NIXON HAS CALLED JOE AZBELL, THE EDITOR FOR THE MONTGOMERY ADVERTISER.
ON SUNDAY, HE'LL BE ISSUING THE HANDBILL ON THE FRONT PAGE OF THE PAPER.
The Montgomery Advertiser
Sunday Morning, December 4, 1955


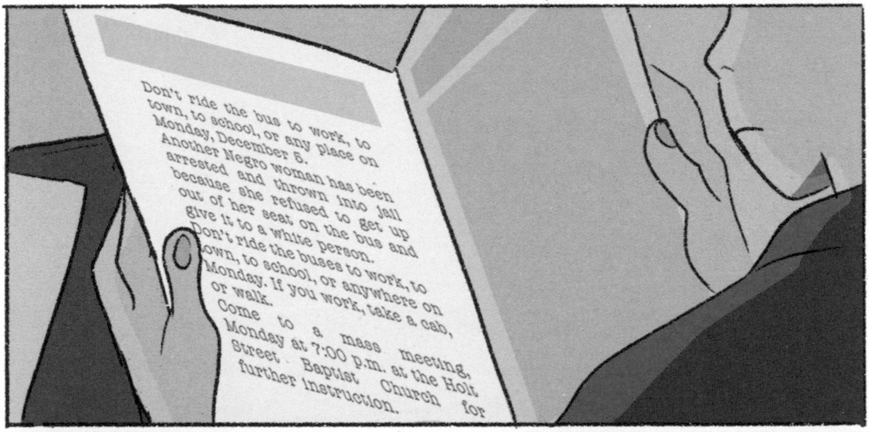

Don't ride the bus to work, to town, to school, or any place on Monday, December 5.
Another Negro woman has been arrested and thrown into jail because she refused to get up out of her seat on the bus and give it to a white person.
Don't ride the buses to work, to town, to school, or anywhere on Monday. If you work, take a cab, or walk.
Come to a mass meeting, Monday at 7:00 p.m. at the Holt Street Baptist Church for further instruction.


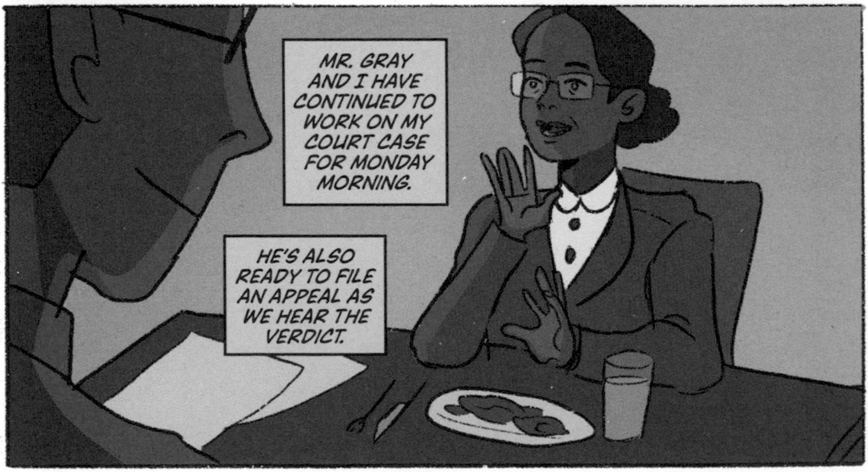

MR. GRAY AND I HAVE CONTINUED TO WORK ON MY COURT CASE FOR MONDAY MORNING.
HE'S ALSO READY TO FILE AN APPEAL AS WE HEAR THE VERDICT.

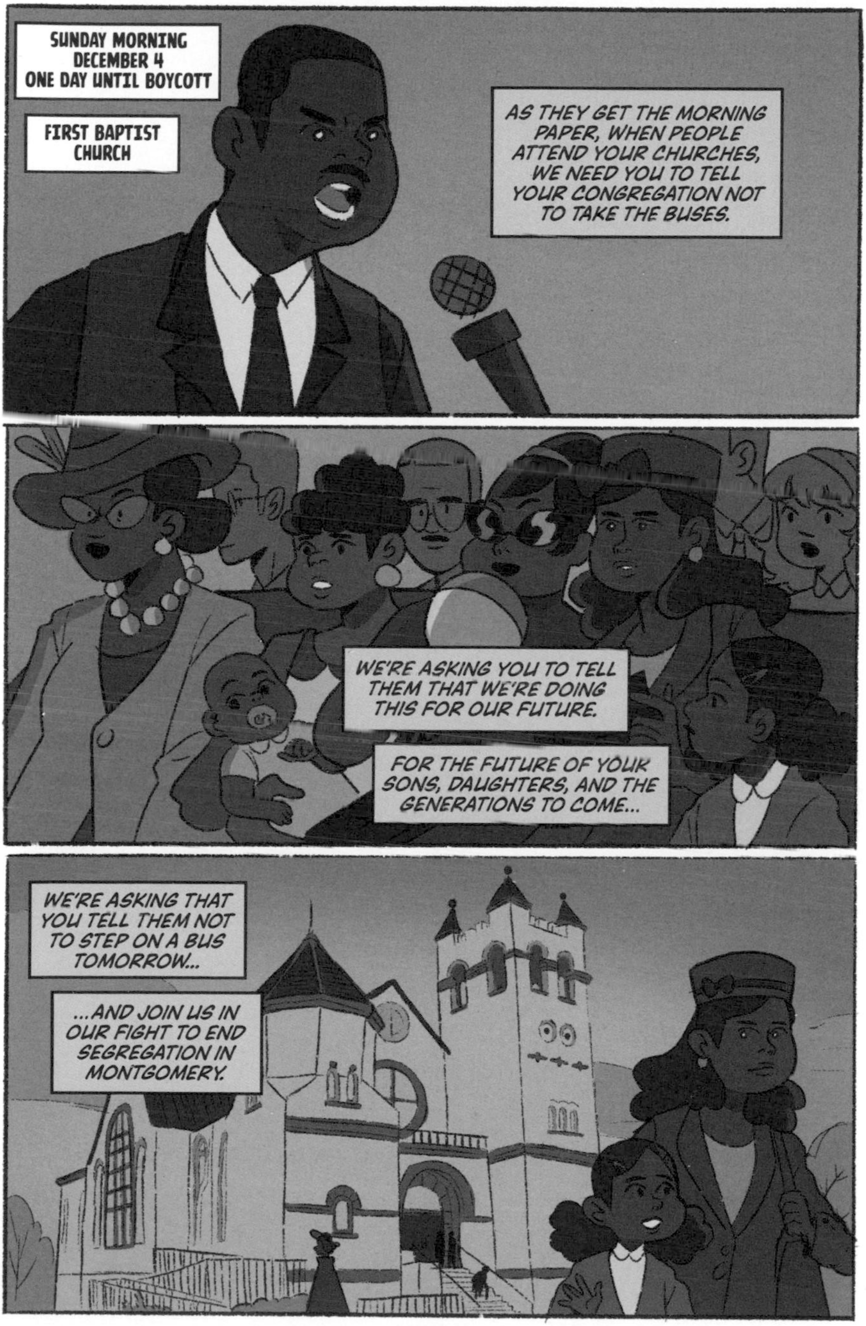
SUNDAY MORNING
DECEMBER 4
ONE DAY UNTIL BOYCOTT
FIRST BAPTIST CHURCH
AS THEY GET THE MORNING PAPER, WHEN PEOPLE ATTEND YOUR CHURCHES, WE NEED YOU TO TELL YOUR CONGREGATION NOT TO TAKE THE BUSES.
WE'RE ASKING YOU TO TELL THEM THAT WE'RE DOING THIS FOR OUR FUTURE.
FOR THE FUTURE OF YOUR SONS, DAUGHTERS, AND THE GENERATIONS TO COME...
WE'RE ASKING THAT YOU TELL THEM NOT TO STEP ON A BUS TOMORROW...
...AND JOIN US IN OUR FIGHT TO END SEGREGATION IN MONTGOMERY.

34

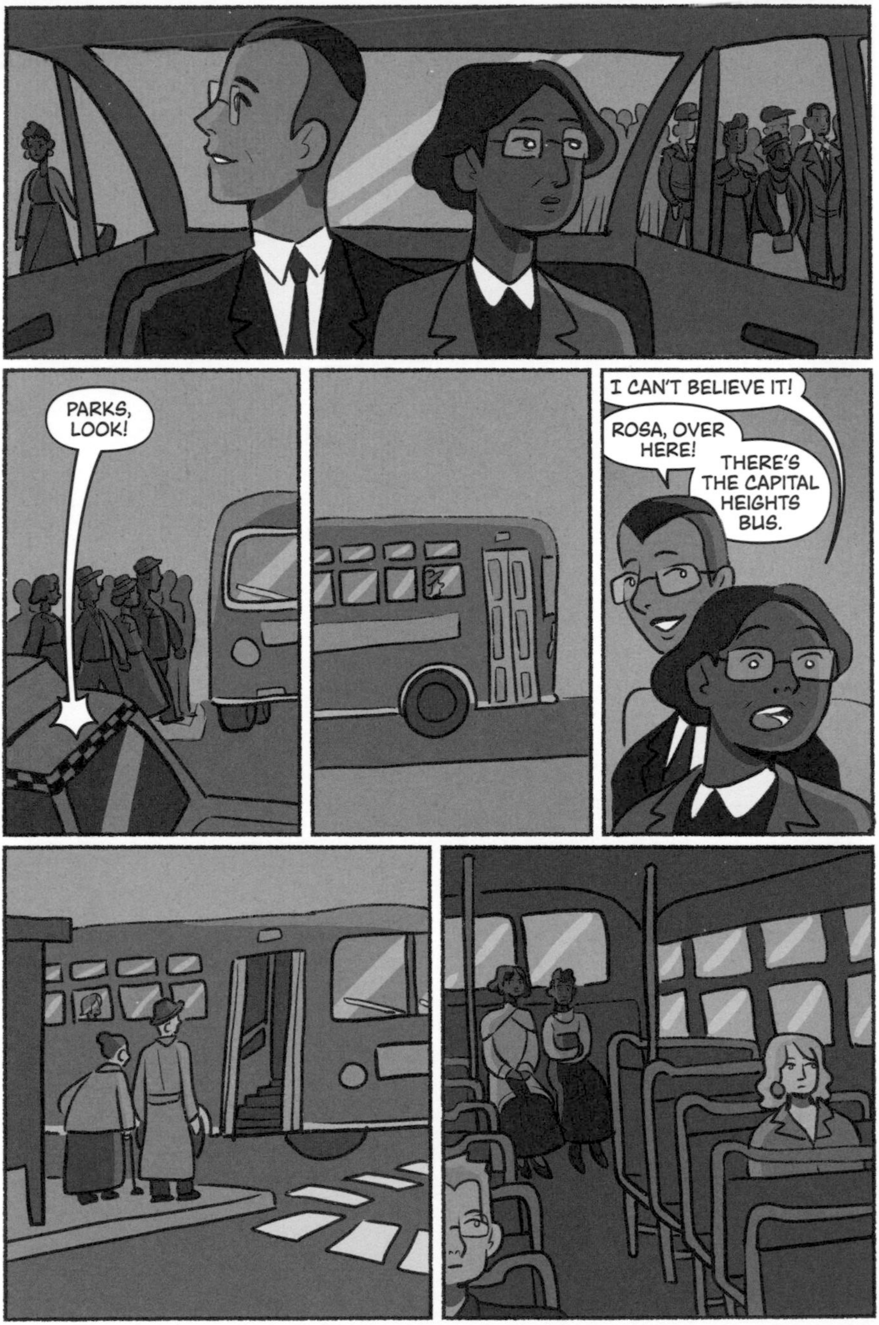
PARKS, LOOK!
I CAN'T BELIEVE IT!
ROSA, OVER HERE!
THERE'S THE CAPITAL HEIGHTS BUS.

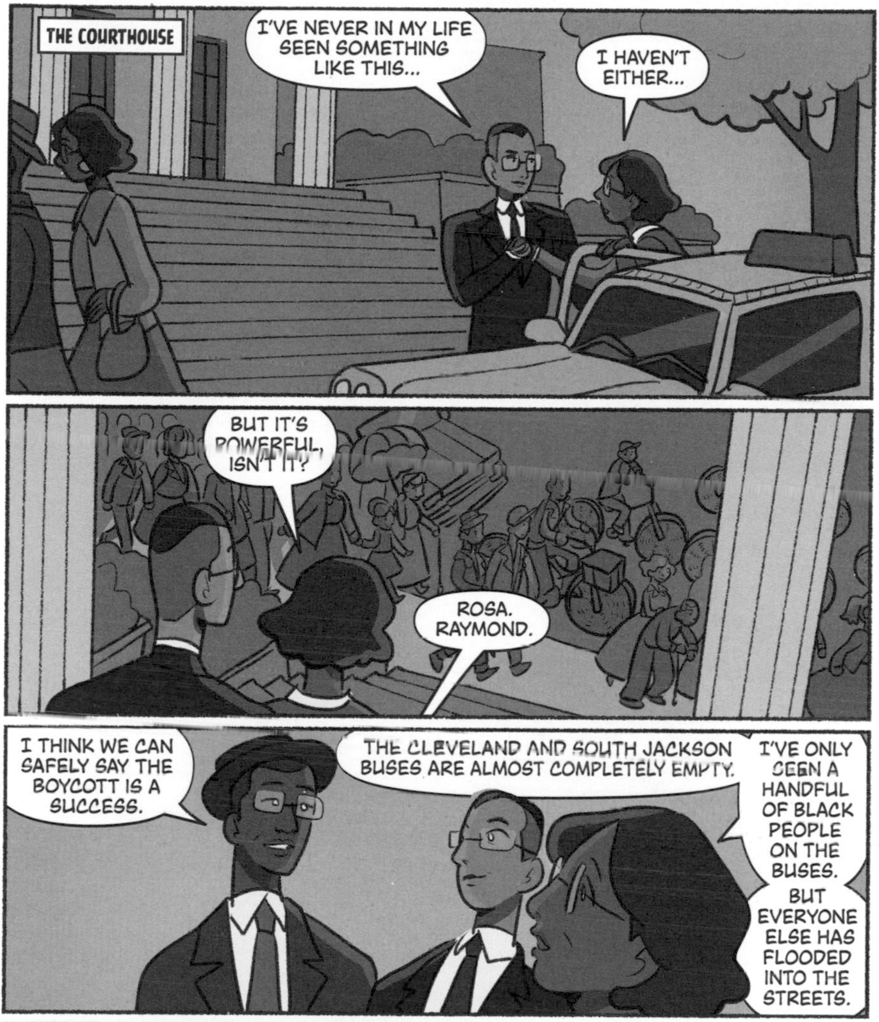
THE COURTHOUSE
I'VE NEVER IN MY LIFE SEEN SOMETHING LIKE THIS...
I HAVEN'T EITHER...
BUT IT'S POWERFUL, ISN'T IT?
ROSA. RAYMOND.
I THINK WE CAN SAFELY SAY THE BOYCOTT IS A SUCCESS.
THE CLEVELAND AND SOUTH JACKSON BUSES ARE ALMOST COMPLETELY EMPTY.
I'VE ONLY SEEN A HANDFUL OF BLACK PEOPLE ON THE BUSES.
BUT EVERYONE ELSE HAS FLOODED INTO THE STREETS.
THAT'S NOT ALL.
ALL ALONG THE STREETS, THERE'S CHANGE HAPPENING.

# Montgomery Improvement Association

The Montgomery Improvement Association, or MIA, was one of the leading organizations in supporting the Montgomery Bus Boycott. Led by Martin Luther King Jr., the MIA was made up of eighteen members and used a nonviolent approach to protest segregation.

The Montgomery Improvement Association helped keep Montgomery informed of what was happening during the boycott. They raised money and collected donated items for protestors, including shoes for those who wore out the soles of theirs from walking. They provided carpooling, which worked as a taxi-like system. Church vans and privately owned vehicles helped anyone get around where they needed to go.

The organization continued to provide help to Black people in Montgomery after the boycott ended. They coordinated people to vote and tried to end segregation in many local schools, parks, and other facilities that Black people weren't allowed to go to. In 1957, the MIA slowly dissolved, but gave way to the Southern Christian Leadership Conference, an organization that still continues to do civil rights work today.

44

45

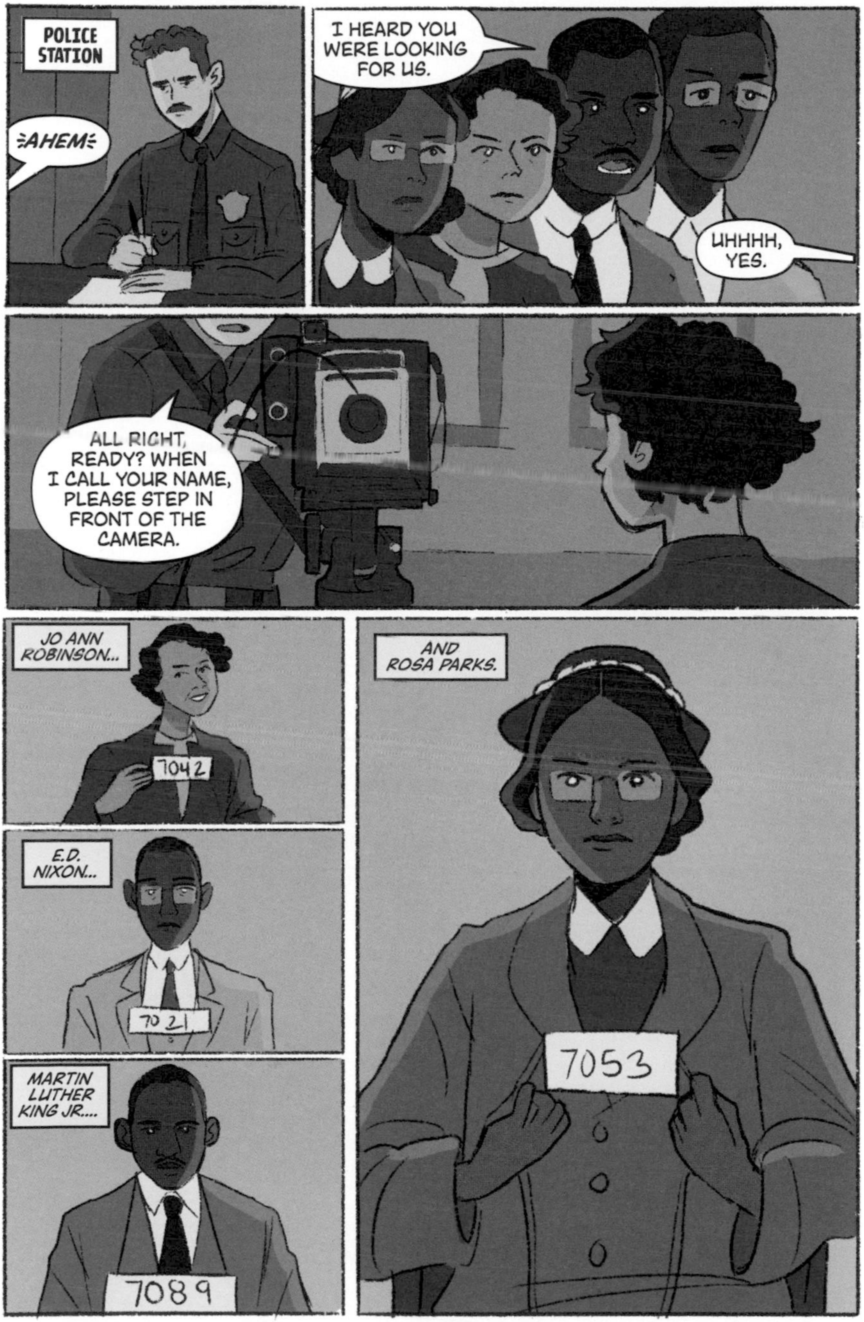
POLICE STATION
AHEM
I HEARD YOU WERE LOOKING FOR US.
UHHHH, YES.
ALL RIGHT, READY? WHEN I CALL YOUR NAME, PLEASE STEP IN FRONT OF THE CAMERA.
JO ANN ROBINSON...
7042
E.D. NIXON...
7021
MARTIN LUTHER KING JR....
7089
AND ROSA PARKS.
7053

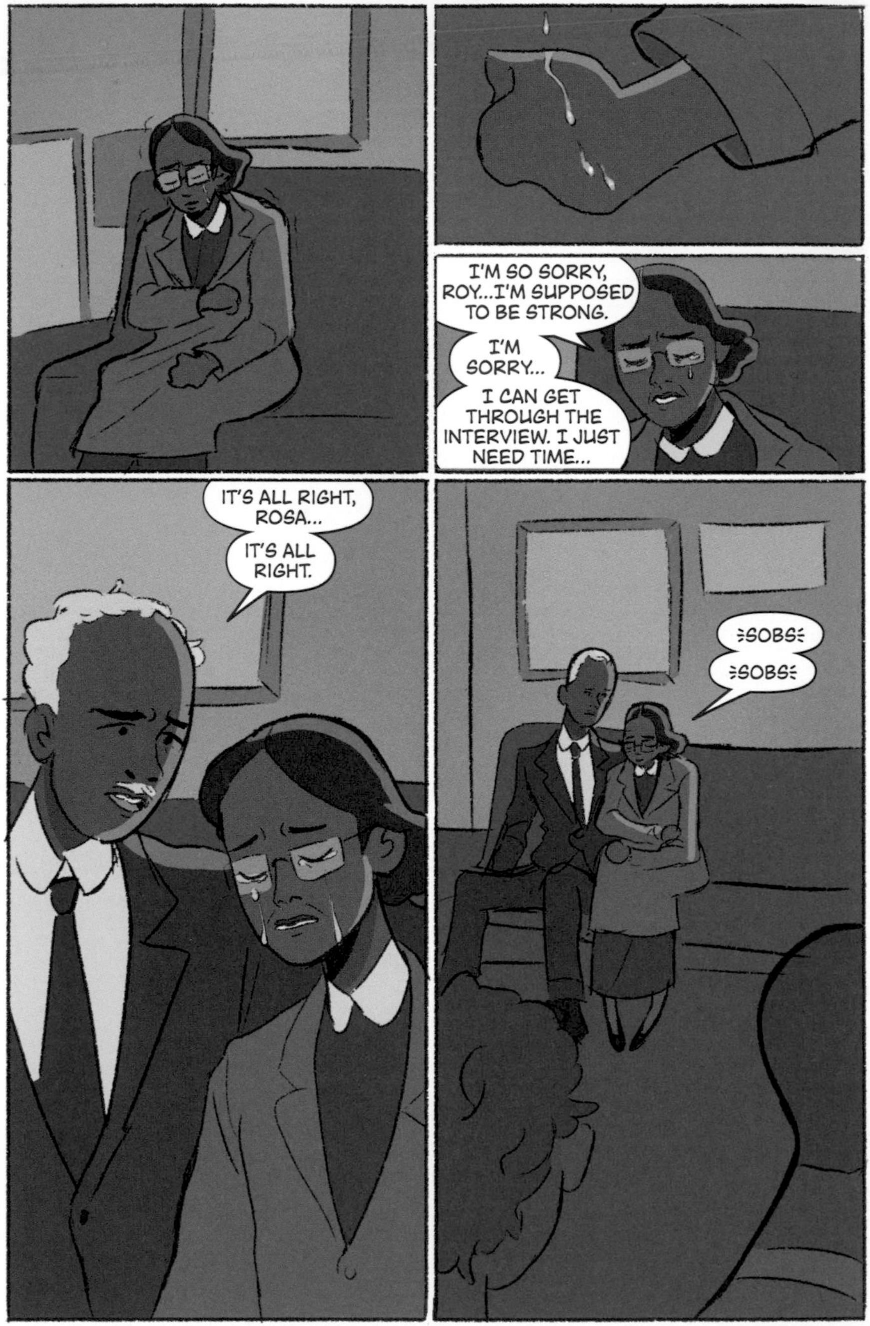
I'M SO SORRY, ROY...I'M SUPPOSED TO BE STRONG.
I'M SORRY...
I CAN GET THROUGH THE INTERVIEW. I JUST NEED TIME...
IT'S ALL RIGHT, ROSA...
IT'S ALL RIGHT.
SOBS
SOBS

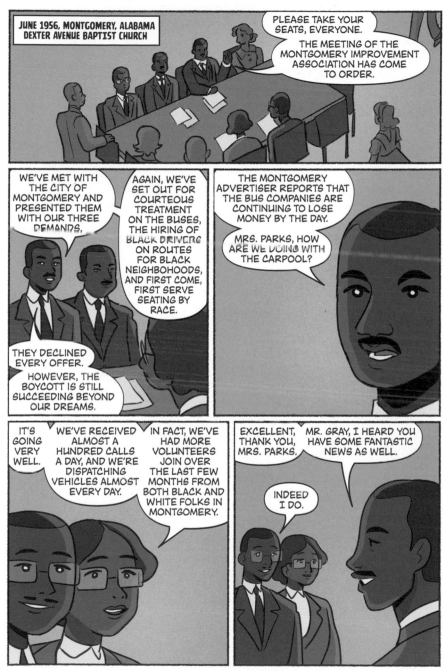

# Claudette Colvin

Born on September 5, 1939, Claudette Colvin is a retired nurse aid and civil rights leader who grew up in Montgomery, Alabama. From a young age, Claudette had a particular interest in activism. She was a good, curious student and an active member of the NAACP youth council.

On March 2, 1955, Claudette, who was fifteen at the time, was arrested for not giving up her seat on a crowded bus to a white passenger. The NAACP thought about representing Claudette as a test case in court, but decided against it because, not long before her court date, she became pregnant. Claudette went to court by herself and was found guilty of violating segregation laws. The courts sentenced her to probation.

In 1956, Colvin became one of the four plaintiffs in the case of *Browder v. Gayle*, which protested segregation on buses in Montgomery, Alabama. Claudette was vital in organizing the fight against segregation during the civil rights movement.

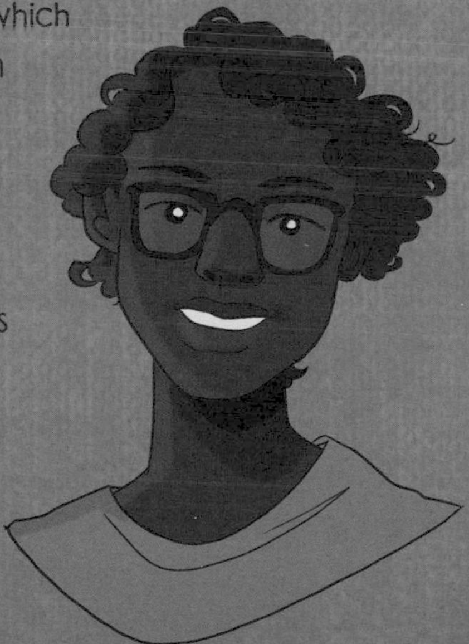

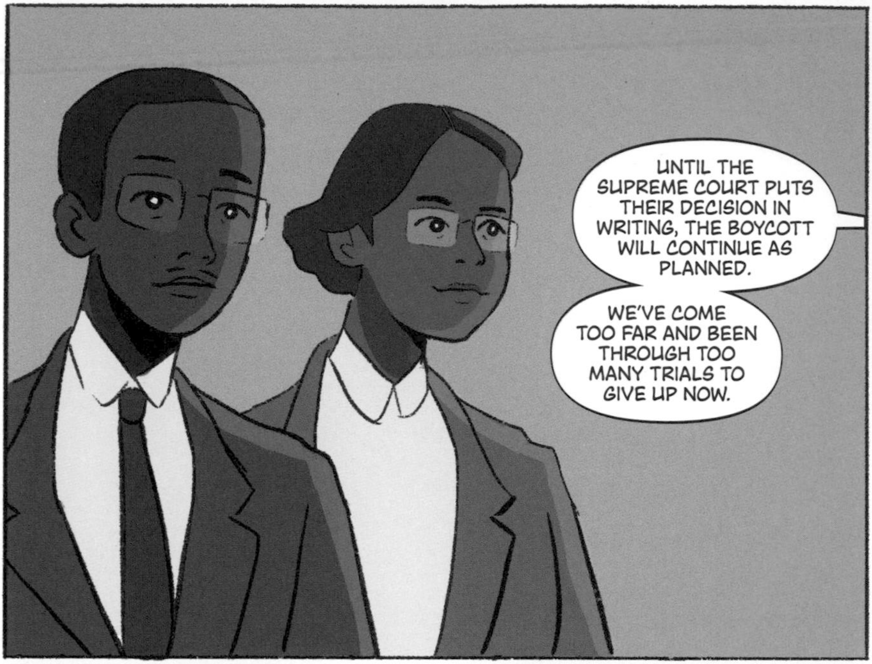
UNTIL THE SUPREME COURT PUTS THEIR DECISION IN WRITING, THE BOYCOTT WILL CONTINUE AS PLANNED.
WE'VE COME TOO FAR AND BEEN THROUGH TOO MANY TRIALS TO GIVE UP NOW.

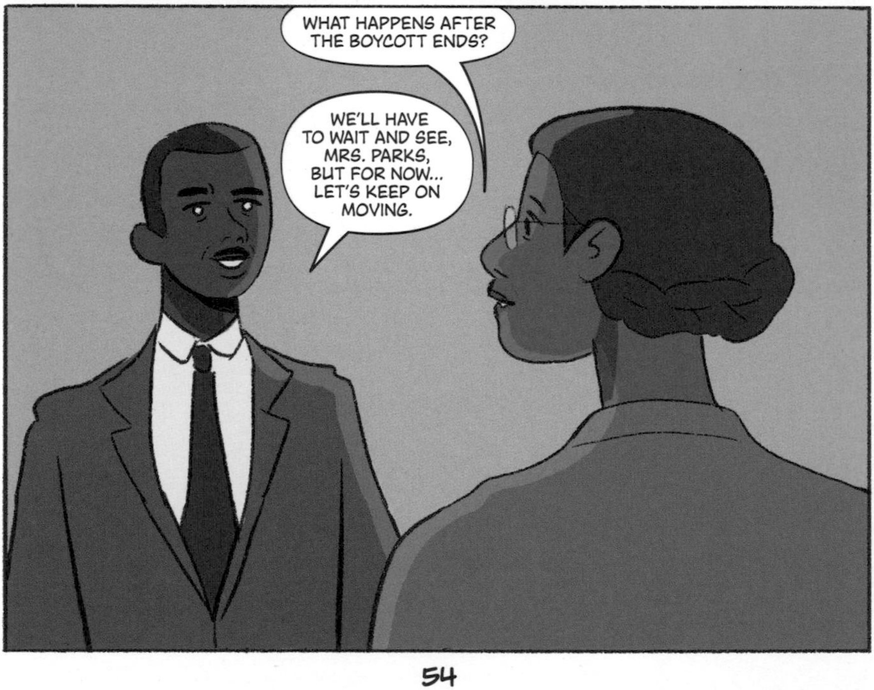
WHAT HAPPENS AFTER THE BOYCOTT ENDS?
WE'LL HAVE TO WAIT AND SEE, MRS. PARKS, BUT FOR NOW... LET'S KEEP ON MOVING.

55

57

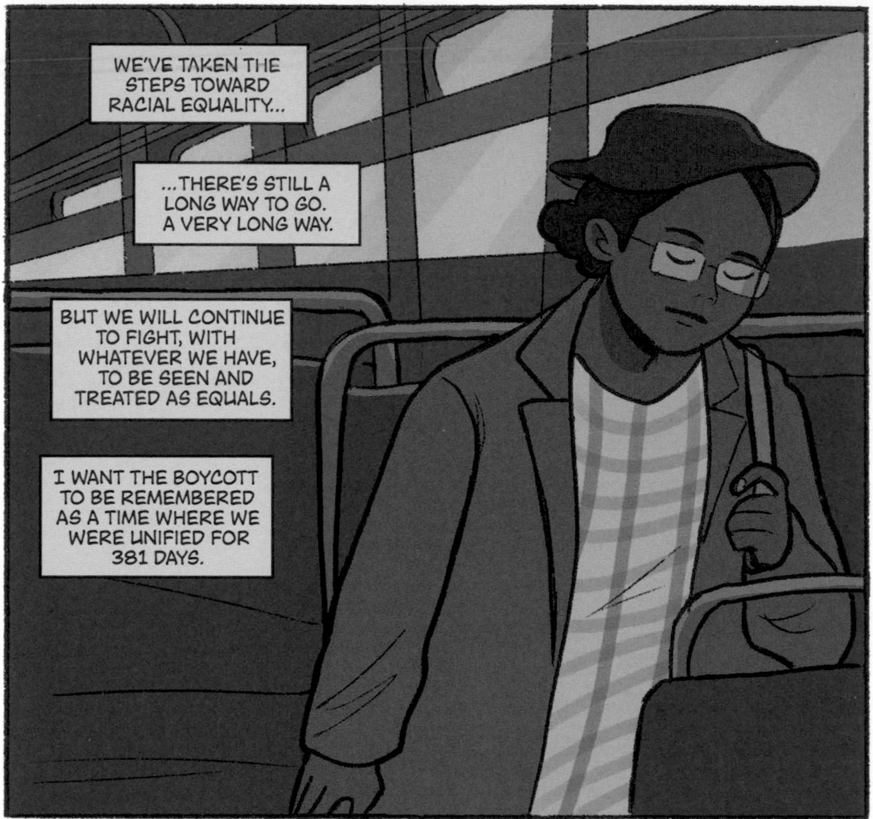
WE'VE TAKEN THE STEPS TOWARD RACIAL EQUALITY...
...THERE'S STILL A LONG WAY TO GO. A VERY LONG WAY.
BUT WE WILL CONTINUE TO FIGHT, WITH WHATEVER WE HAVE, TO BE SEEN AND TREATED AS EQUALS.
I WANT THE BOYCOTT TO BE REMEMBERED AS A TIME WHERE WE WERE UNIFIED FOR 381 DAYS.

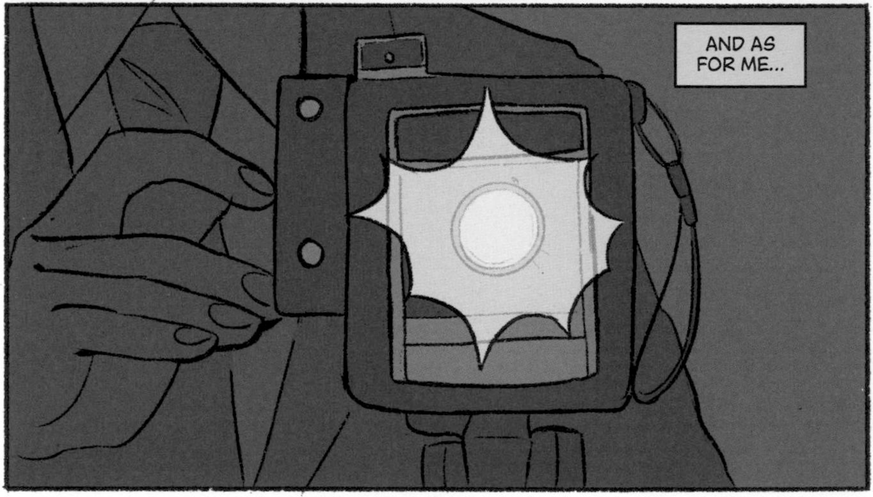
AND AS FOR ME...

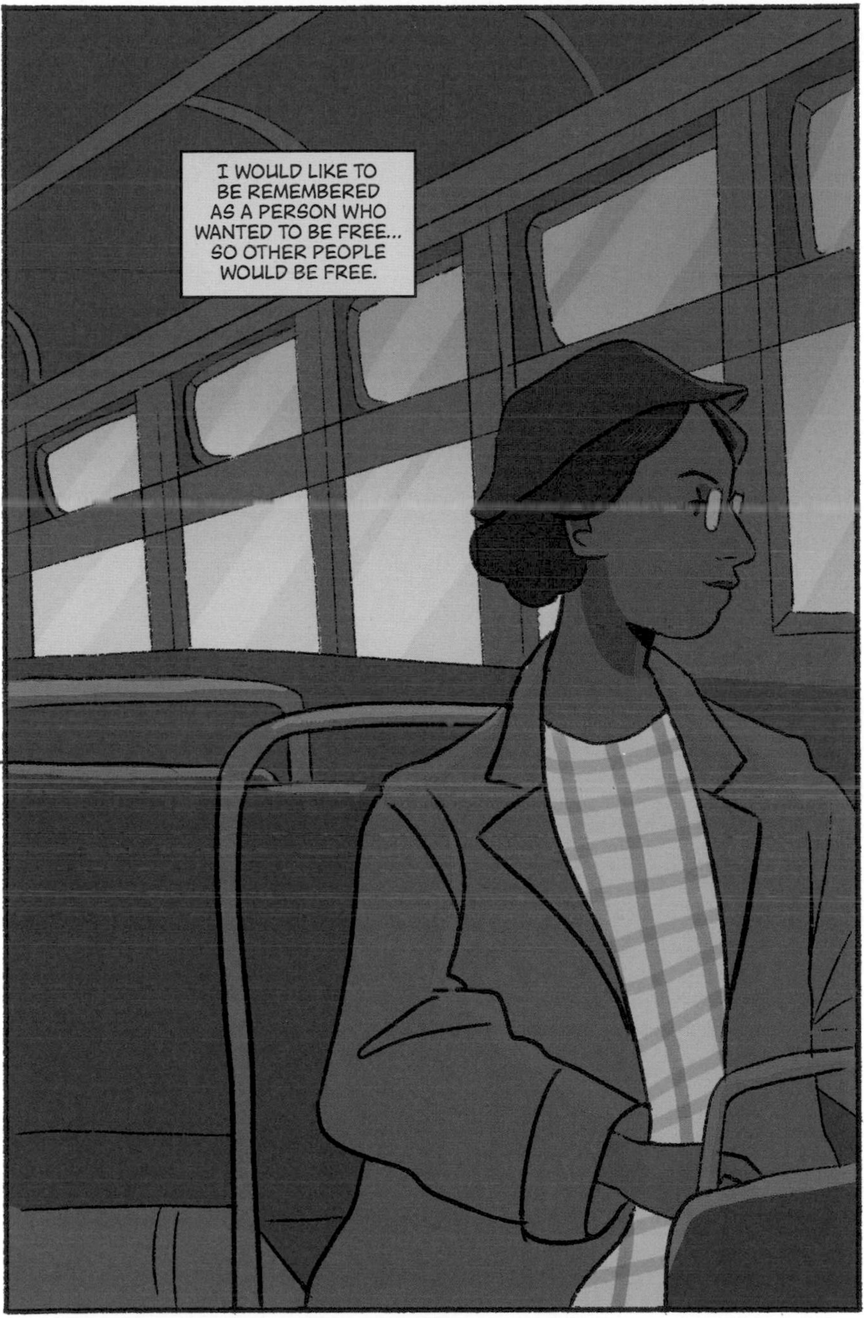
I WOULD LIKE TO BE REMEMBERED AS A PERSON WHO WANTED TO BE FREE... SO OTHER PEOPLE WOULD BE FREE.

# Conclusion

After the Montgomery Bus Boycott, Rosa Parks moved out of the spotlight, but things were still hard for her and her family. Rosa and Raymond continued to receive threats and struggled to get any type of work. They had to make a tough decision: After living in Montgomery, Alabama, for most of their lives, Rosa, Raymond, and Rosa's mother, Leona, decided to move to Detroit, Michigan, to live near Rosa's brother, Sylvester McCauley.

The move from Montgomery was difficult, but it didn't stop Rosa from advocating for civil rights. Rosa worked with the local Detroit chapter of the NAACP and gave many speeches in churches and schools about her experiences. She walked in the March on Washington in 1963 and watched Martin Luther King Jr. give his "I Have a Dream" speech that same year. Two years later, she participated in the Selma to Montgomery March, a protest that helped allow Black people to vote.

In 1987, at seventy-four years old, she cofounded the Rosa and Raymond Parks Institute for Self-Development in Detroit with Elaine Eason Steele. The institute became a place to educate young people to better themselves and their community. The NAACP awarded Rosa the Spingarn Medal in 1979. She then received the Presidential Medal of Freedom in 1996 and the Congressional Gold Medal in 1999. She was named one of the most important people of the twentieth century in *Time* magazine. Rosa also wrote four books, including her 1992 memoir, with the help of author Jim Haskins, titled *Rosa Parks: My Story*.

On October 24, 2005, Rosa Parks died of natural causes at ninety-two. She was laid to rest in the Capitol building in Washington, DC, the first woman to have that honor. Rosa Parks spent her life fighting for civil rights—from standing up for herself on the bus to marching with thousands to help gain Black Americans the right to vote. Behind every movement, there's someone who lights the spark. Rosa lit the match when she stood her ground that day at the Cleveland Avenue bus stop. And the rest? Fireworks.

# Timeline of Rosa Parks's Life

1913 — Rosa Louise McCauley is born in Tuskegee, Alabama

1932 — Marries Raymond Parks

1943 — Becomes secretary of the Montgomery chapter of the NAACP

1955 — Arrested for not giving her seat up to a white man; Montgomery Bus Boycott begins

— Rosa Parks's trial begins, and she's found guilty

1956 — In February, Martin Luther King Jr., Rosa Parks, E.D. Nixon, Jo Ann Robinson, and others are arrested for violating the state law against boycotting

— In November, US Supreme Court sides with Aurelia Browder in *Browder v. Gayle*; saying that segregation on buses is unconstitutional

1957 — Rosa, Raymond, and Leona move to Detroit

1965 — In March, Selma to Montgomery March begins

— President Lyndon B. Johnson signs the Voting Rights Act of 1965 into law

1975 — Rosa Parks returns for the 20th anniversary of the Montgomery Bus Boycott

1979 — The NAACP gives Rosa the Spingarn Medal

1996 — Receives the Presidential Medal of Freedom

1999 — Receives the Congressional Gold Medal of Honor

2005 — Dies of natural causes at age ninety-two

# Bibliography

**\*Books for young readers**

Brinkley, Douglas. *Rosa Parks: A Life.* New York: Penguin Books, 2005.

\*Freedman, Russell. *Freedom Walkers: The Story of the Montgomery Bus Boycott.* New York: Holiday House, 2009.

\*McDonough, Yona Zeldis. *Who Was Rosa Parks?* New York: Penguin Workshop, 2010.

"Montgomery Bus Boycott." History.com, A&E Networks, February 3, 2010. https://www.history.com/topics/black-history/montgomery-bus-boycott.

\*Parks, Rosa, with Jim Haskins. *Rosa Parks: My Story.* New York: Dial Books, 1992.

\*Pinkney, Andrea Davis, and Brian Pinkney. *Boycott Blues: How Rosa Parks Inspired a Nation.* New York: Greenwillow Books, 2008.

Robinson, Jo Ann, with David J. Garrow. *Montgomery Bus Boycott and the Women Who Started It: The Memoir of Jo Ann Gibson Robinson.* Knoxville, TN: University of Tennessee Press, 1987.

"Rosa Parks." Biography.com, A&E Networks, February 4, 2020. www.biography.com/activist/rosa-parks.

"Rosa Parks." History.com, A&E Networks, November 9, 2009. www.history.com/topics/black-history/rosa-parks.

\*Summer, L.S. *Rosa Parks: Journey to Freedom.* North Mankato, MN: The Child's World, 2000.

\*Time for Kids. *Heroes of Black History.* New York: Liberty Street (Time Inc. Books), 2017.

## ABOUT THE CREATORS

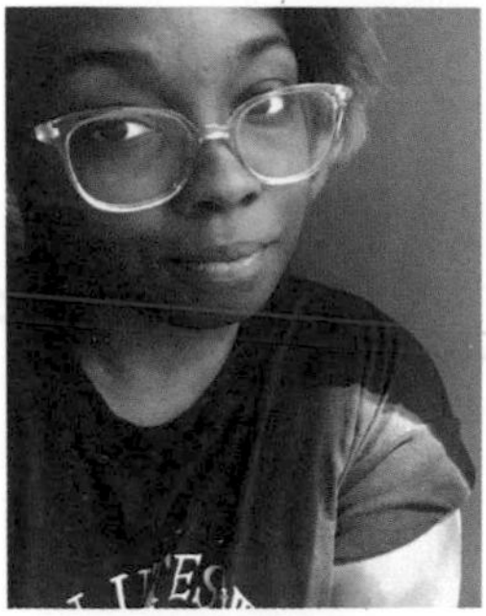

**Insha Fitzpatrick** is a New Jersey-based writer and editor. She's the founder of DIS/MEMBER, a horror genre website, and cowriter of middle-grade graphic novel series *Oh My Gods!* (Etch, 2021). Please talk to her about spooky movies, true crime, or Rod Serling's *Twilight Zone*.

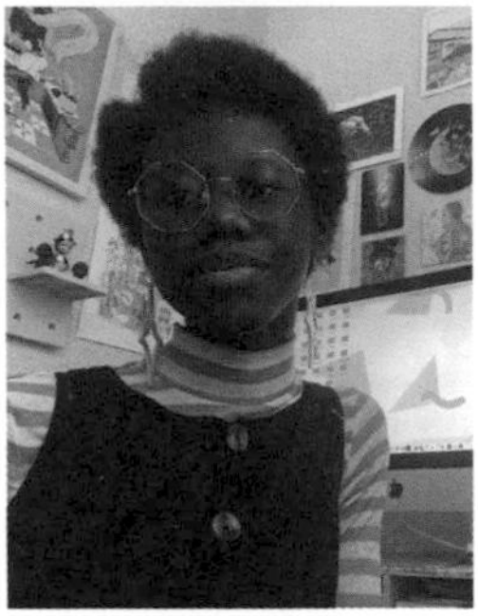

**Abelle Hayford** is a Ghanaian American illustrator, character designer, and color stylist. Their past clients include Warner Bros., *New York Times*, Penguin Random House, Simon & Schuster, and the *New Yorker*. Social media has played a huge role in Abelle's artistic growth, and they use their social media to share their art to others while also promoting other marginalized artists. In this effort, Abelle organized #Drawingwhileblack, a viral hashtag to celebrate and promote Black artists around the world!

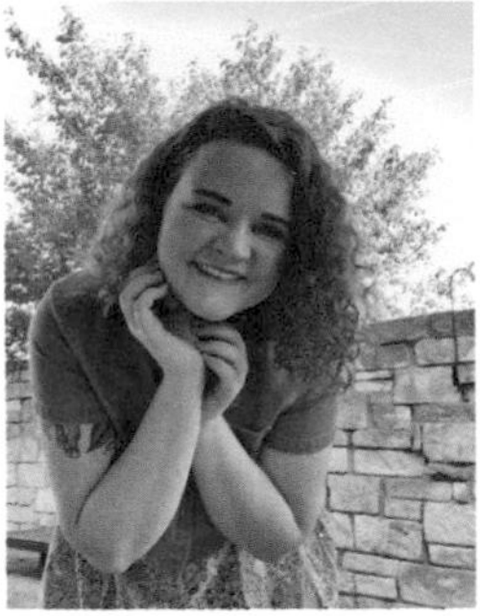

**Hanna Schroy** is an Austin-based cartoonist and illustrator. She is the creator of *Last Dance* (Iron Circus Comics, 2021) and a contributor in the anthology *Girls! Girls! Girls!* curated by Alex Perkins.